# The Bedford Guide for Writing Tutors

## Fifth Edition

**Leigh Ryan**

University of Maryland, College Park

**Lisa Zimmerelli**

University of Maryland University College

**Bedford / St. Martin's**
Boston ◆ New York

Manufactured in the United States of America.
3   2   1   0
e   d   c   b

*Editorial Offices:* Bedford/St. Martin's
75 Arlington Street, Boston, MA 02116
(617-399-4000)

ISBN-10: 0–312–56673–5
ISBN-13: 978–0–312–56673–9

# Preface for
# Writing Center Directors

In my early years of directing a writing center, I longed for a single, short book that my tutors and I could learn from, one that could serve as a resource for tutoring information and techniques. Though I wasn't trying to make composition teachers out of engineering or psychology or dance majors, I did want the tutors to acquire some knowledge of the writing process as well as some strategies that they could use as they worked with students. Because the book didn't exist, I gathered articles and excerpts that we read and discussed. I created and borrowed assignments and exercises to help tutors learn and practice skills. And, I tried to create an environment in which we could share our experiences and learn from one another.

Writing the first edition of *The Bedford Guide for Writing Tutors* gave me the chance to create that short book, one that discusses how tutoring fits into the writing process; offers tutors suggestions and strategies to help students improve their writing; and discusses specific kinds of writers, situations, and assignments that tutors are apt to encounter. It invites tutors to examine and consider their tutoring roles, and it reminds them that they are professionals who are working with writers. Subsequent editions allowed for refining information, adding assignments and activities, and including discussions about the increasing impact of technology on tutoring.

With the fourth edition, I asked my former assistant director Lisa Zimmerelli to collaborate with me. An outstanding teacher, administrator, and tutor—both face-to-face and online—her assistance has been invaluable. Our collaboration often resembled tutoring sessions as we posed questions for one another about our audience, purpose, content, phrasing, and word choices. Working with Lisa reminded me anew of Kenneth Bruffee and the social nature of tutoring.[1]

Both the fourth and fifth editions reflect the ever-increasing impact of technology on writing, tutoring, and learning. The fifth edition treats tutoring and technology more fully and incorporates suggestions for best practices in synchronous and asynchronous online tutoring throughout the text. We also carefully edited this edition with an eye toward the growing international community of writing centers, a very exciting phenomenon. In an effort to keep our selected bibliography more up-to-date, we have moved it online: you will find it at www.hackerhandbooks.com/bedhandbook.

---

[1]Kenneth Bruffee. "Collaborative Learning and the 'Conversation of Mankind.'" *College English* 46 (November 1984): 635–52.

We believe that writing center administrators everywhere will find this book useful. Staff, clients, services, and missions vary from one writing center to another. We hope that administrators will adapt this guide to the unique needs of their writing centers, spending more or less time on specific sections and appropriate exercises and supplementing with articles, handouts, and exercises they may already use.

## How to Use this Guide

*The Bedford Guide for Writing Tutors* offers advice and suggestions to writing tutors. Reviewers and users continually acknowledge its brevity and practicality as its chief virtues, even as they sometimes request more content in some areas.

Most of us—administrators and tutors—view writing centers through the lens of what we know. Not surprisingly, that's our own writing centers. Just listen to presenters at conferences, directors and tutors alike, as they refer to a writing course simply as "English 108," assuming that everyone will know what they mean, or use the term "Writing Central" or the "Café"—the name of their writing center—as if everyone will automatically recognize that as the writing center.

Writing centers do vary, and significantly. Some offer only face-to-face sessions; others provide only online tutoring, which may be synchronous, asynchronous, or a blend of the two; and some offer a mix of face-to-face and online tutoring. Staff may be peer tutors, graduate students, professional tutors, faculty, or even community volunteers, and the population served is typically unique to a writing center's particular college or institution: undergraduates, graduate students, faculty, staff, community writers, or some combination thereof. Services include not only tutoring but also workshops, grammar hotlines, chats, and online files of handouts. Hours vary, with services available days, evenings, or even on weekends. Locations for sessions—classrooms, libraries, dormitories—vary as well.

*The Bedford Guide for Writing Tutors* intends to be a general guide for writing tutors across the spectrum of writing centers—face-to-face and online. Furthermore, while its main focus may be writing center tutors, it attempts to accommodate individual tutors as well. Since particular institutions serve specific populations, we encourage you to supplement the guide with readings and online resources that focus on the needs of your clients.

What also varies, and significantly, is tutor training, and for that reason we have tried to provide a wide variety of exercises. Our hope is to accommodate large classes of twenty and small classes of one or two, as well as tutors at large state universities, small private institutions, community colleges, and high schools. The exercises in this guide connect directly with acquiring and practicing tutoring skills and strategies. Many training programs require tutors to maintain a journal or participate in online conversations, so we've included suggestions for those activities. We've also included typical assignments in which tutors investigate and discuss their own writing processes. Because some new tutors haven't been tutored themselves, we suggest that they seek tutoring as they complete the assignment. Other exercises ask tutors to investigate how writing is taught at their school as well as to practice and discuss tutoring tools and strategies. Later activities ask tutors to reflect on and synthesize their tutoring experiences. For use with larger classes, some exercises include many options; if your class is small, you might limit those options by asking tutors to go through only a few of the exercises. We invite you to choose, rearrange, adapt, and tailor these exercises to your needs and those of your writing center. You might, for example, choose to ask tutors to complete some exercises before reading a chapter in order to get them thinking about issues and to give them a reason to read more carefully.

Because tutors work with writers rather than just with papers, we include no complete sample texts of student writing. While tutors could discuss how they might begin a session with a particular paper or what they might focus on, without a writer to respond, tutors can only speculate — an arrangement that does not represent the reality of a tutoring session. We also believe that discussing how isolated papers might be improved encourages tutors to correct the writing rather than to ask the questions that will guide the writer to a better understanding of the composition process.

## Acknowledgments

For this edition, Lisa and I turned to several colleagues for advice and suggestions, and we are grateful to them for their wisdom and guidance: Althea Allard, Community College of Rhode Island; Valerie Balester, Texas A & M University; Sarah Baker, George Mason University; Gerd Bräuer, University of Education Freiburg/Germany; Tammy Conard-Salvo, Purdue University; Mary Deane, Coventry University; Tom Deans, University of Connecticut; Michele Eodice, University of Oklahoma; Shareen Grogan, National University; Eiman Hajabbassi, George Mason University; Dean Hinnen, University of Texas at Arlington; Susan Mueller, St. Louis College of Pharmacy; Manuel Perea, Pasadena City College; Herbert Shapiro, Empire State College SUNY; Mary Beth Simmons, Villanova University; Neil Ward, Empire State College SUNY; and our anonymous reviewer from Virginia Commonwealth University.

For their helpful suggestions for previous editions, we also wish to thank the following reviewers: Sonja S. Bagby, State University of West Georgia; Mary Jo Berger, Randolph-Macon College; Eric Crump, University of Missouri, Columbia; Sharifa Daniels, Stellenbosch University (South Africa); Francis DeBernardo, University of Maryland; Teagan Decker, University of Washington; Geraldine C. Fisher, Washington College; Jack Folsom, Montana State University; Donald Houch, University of Maryland, University College; John Hyman, American University; Barbara Jensen, Modesto

Junior College; Debbie Kimberlin, University of Nebraska at Omaha; Kate Mele, Roger Williams College; Jon Olson, Oregon State University; Rose Richards, Stellenbosch University (South Africa); Becky Rickly, University of Michigan at Ann Arbor; Suzanne Swiderski, Loras College; Heather Urschel-Speir, Tacoma Community College; Greg Wahl, Montgomery College, Tacoma Park; Julie Warmke-Robitaille, Santa Fe Community College; and Molly Wingate, The Colorado College.

Thanks, too, to the late Diana Hacker for her wisdom, guidance, and support. A special note of thanks to Colleen Ryan Leonard, Matt Ryan, and John Zimmerelli, each of whom patiently listened, read, and advised through drafts.

Thanks again to those at Bedford/St. Martin's: Chuck Christensen, Joan Feinberg, and most especially, Alicia Young for her expert guidance. Lisa and I are also grateful to Elizabeth Schaaf and Lindsay DiGianvittorio, who carefully oversaw the production of the fifth edition, and to Mary Lou Wilshaw-Watts for her skillful copyediting.

Most especially, Leigh wishes to acknowledge and thank her assistant directors, former and current: Rebecca Spracklin, Charles Magnetti, Francis DeBernardo, Melinda Schwenk, Jenny Steinberg, Traci Abbott, Rachel Kovacs, Patricia Lissner, Eleanor Shevlin, Greg Wahl, Sara Glasgow, Elliot Wright, Soo Jung Suh, Wendy Hayden, Nancy Comorau, helen Devinney, Heather Blain, Tyler Caroline Mills, Heather Brown, and Joseph Kautzer. Lisa wishes to acknowledge and thank her lead advisor, John Whitcraft, and senior advisor, David Taylor. Lisa and I especially thank all the tutors who through the years have worked at the University of Maryland's Writing Center and the University of Maryland University College's online Effective Writing Center. We have learned—and continue to learn—so much from all of you.

Leigh Ryan
University of Maryland, College Park

Lisa Zimmerelli
University of Maryland University College

# Introduction for Tutors

If we could tell you only one thing about tutoring, it's that your real task is to change the way students go about writing. That may not be what you think about tutoring now, and it's certainly not what most students have in mind when they come to a writing center. Often, students' thoughts are something like the following:

1. Visit writing center with rough draft because I want a good grade.
2. Tutor tells me where and how to fix what either of us identifies as problems.
3. I fix problems.
4. I get a good grade.

Consequently, new tutors commonly feel enormous pressure to "perfect" a paper or to tutor to the student's highest expectations. Both of us, however, have stories that suggest alternative viewpoints on your new role as a writing tutor.

**Leigh:** One summer, Annie, a bright graduate student who wrote well, came to tutor in the writing center. With no formal tutor training offered in the summer, we settled on an independent course of study. We met several times to discuss tutoring strategies, the university's writing programs, and some articles about writing and tutoring. But even after several weeks, she couldn't seem to settle comfortably into tutoring. She often ran over the fifty-minute time limit on sessions as she tried to cover every problem that she encountered in a paper. Instead of seeming relaxed as she worked with writers, she was usually harried and breathless. Worst of all, she didn't seem to be enjoying herself.

We talked frequently and at length, analyzing what she'd done in tutoring sessions. Finally one day, Annie blurted out, "It's just that I think every student should leave here with an A paper or I'm not a good tutor. That's what's wrong. And I have to get over that." She was right. It didn't happen immediately, but Annie finally came to recognize what her job as a writing tutor really involved: She was someone who could help writers sort through their ideas, clarify their thoughts, and then communicate them effectively to an audience. Perhaps most important, she was also someone who could show students strategies for going about this messy task of writing more easily—for particular assignments and for all future ones. All of us, even those who write well, can use an ally like Annie when we write.

**Lisa:** Jason, a relatively new tutor, came to me midsemester frustrated about his tutoring experiences thus far. He explained, "These students just don't get it. They don't understand what I'm here to do. They keep expecting me to just fix things in their papers, and they get mad when I refuse to do that."

I asked him to tell me about a typical tutoring session that he might have with a student. Jason told me that he started by telling the student what he wasn't there to do—edit, proofread, or copyedit. Then, he had the student read the paper aloud. He followed by asking the student what she or he thought needed improvement. If the student asked him for advice, he explained that it was not his job to fix the paper for the student. "I do what you tell us to do," he said. "I never write on students' papers, and I always try to get the students to revise their papers completely on their own."

Jason thought that he had the students' best interests at heart and that the only way to help writers was to be completely hands-off. "Have you ever tried something new?" I asked him. "Sure," he said, "skydiving." I asked him to think back to the first time he took a jump. How did he feel? What kind of guidance did he need in order to feel safe and confident enough to jump? Wasn't it sometimes pretty explicit guidance? I then suggested that this may be how a student feels approaching him for writing help.

On the other end of the spectrum was Sheela, an online writing tutor. I was reviewing time sheets and noticed that Sheela was averaging four hours per asynchronous advising session. I looked over her advice. She was providing ten pages of advice for three- or four-page papers. The advice was solid, and she certainly was not "editing" or "proofreading" the student's paper, but it was overwhelming, to say the least.

Sheela told me that because she did not have the benefit of talking to the student for these asynchronous sessions, she felt she had to address every problem. If she saw one comma error, she offered advice on commas, complete with two examples and three outside references. Sheela and I talked about prioritizing. We also talked about how asynchronous sessions do not have to be seen as a "one shot deal" with students. We can encourage students to come back to the writing center; we can point out some other areas for improvement without expanding on each one in explicit detail.

How we go about tutoring—doing what Annie, Jason, and Sheela finally understood as their real job—is the subject of *The Bedford Guide for Writing Tutors*. The book's nine chapters discuss the writing process and strategies for helping students with it. They provide principles and strategies for tutors who work in a variety of contexts—in large or small, college or high school, online or face-to-face writing centers. Each chapter offers practical advice for tutoring in general as well as for dealing with specific kinds of students and assignments.

In order to give you opportunities to discover more about writing and tutoring and to practice what you've learned, *The Bedford Guide for Writing Tutors* also includes several sets of chapter exercises. Many of these exercises work best in a class where tutors can share what they discover, but if you are using this book on your own, you might want to respond to exercises in a journal.

This book also addresses how technology influences the ways we talk about writing and work with students in tutoring sessions. Nearly every writing center has several computers, and many writing centers now have an online writing lab (OWL) and/or offer online tutoring. Because technology has a critical place in writing pedagogy, this book will help familiarize you with effective ways to incorporate technology into your tutoring.

Our hope is that *The Bedford Guide for Writing Tutors* helps you become an increasingly confident and competent writing tutor. We also hope that, as you do so, you will come to find tutoring as exciting and rewarding as we do.

# Contents

Preface for Writing Center Directors    iii

Introduction for Tutors    vii

## 1    The Writing Center as a Workplace    1

Professionalism toward the Writer    1

Professionalism toward Other Tutors    2

Professionalism toward Teachers    3

EXERCISES FOR GETTING STARTED    4

EXERCISE 1A    Keeping a Personal Tutoring Journal    4

EXERCISE 1B    Participating in Discussion Forums    5

EXERCISE 1C    Learning about Writing Center History    5

## 2    The Writing Process    6

A General Guide to Stages of the Writing Process    8

Prewriting    8

Writing    9

Revising and Editing    9

■ Stages of the Writing Process    10

EXERCISES FOR EXPLORING THE WRITING PROCESS    11

EXERCISE 2A    Comparing Writing Guides and Handbooks    11

EXERCISE 2B    Teaching Writing    11

EXERCISE 2C    Talking about the Writing Process    12

EXERCISE 2D    Talking about the Writing Process at Your School    13

EXERCISES FOR REFLECTING ON YOUR WRITING PROCESS    13

EXERCISE 2E    Reflecting on Writing    14

EXERCISE 2F    Sharing Your Writing Process    15

EXERCISE 2G    Reflecting on Being Tutored    16

## 3    Inside the Tutoring Session    17

Getting Started    17

Setting the Agenda    19

Three Effective, Powerful Tools  21
  Active Listening  22
  ■ A Note about Asking Questions  24
  Facilitating  24
  Silence and Wait Time  27
  Wrapping Up a Session  28

The Many Hats Tutors Wear  28
  The Ally  28
  The Coach  29
  The Commentator  29
  The Collaborator  29
  The Writing "Expert"  30
  The Learner  30
  The Counselor  31

When Is a Tutor Not a Tutor?  31

**EXERCISES FOR EXPLORING THE ROLES TUTORS PLAY**  32
EXERCISE 3A   Exploring Tutors' Roles  32
EXERCISE 3B   Observing Tutors' and Writers' Body Language  32
EXERCISE 3C   Observing Tutoring Sessions  32

**EXERCISES FOR PRACTICING TUTORING TECHNIQUES**  32
EXERCISE 3D   Role-Playing the Tutoring Session  33
  ■ Tutor Observation Sheet  34
EXERCISE 3E   Role-Playing Tutor Strategies in the Prewriting Stage  38

## 4   Helping Writers throughout the Writing Process   41

Prewriting  41
  Finding and Exploring a Topic  41
  Planning to Write  45
  Working with a Text at a Computer  46

Writing, Revising, and Editing  48
  Making Global Revisions  48
  ■ Saving Multiple Drafts  51
  Making Sentence-Level Revisions  51
  Editing for Grammar, Punctuation, and Mechanics  52

Using a Handbook  54

Coping with the Long Paper  54

**EXERCISES FOR USING WRITING REFERENCES**  56
EXERCISE 4A   Exploring Prewriting Strategies  56
EXERCISE 4B   Developing a Handout  56
EXERCISE 4C   Working with Handbooks and Other References  56

**5  The Writers You Tutor  58**

Learning Styles  59
  Some Helpful Strategies  60
Student Concerns  61
The Writer with Writing Anxiety  61
The Writer with Basic Writing Skills  63
The Second Language Writer  65
The Writer with a Learning Disability  70
The Adult Learner  71

EXERCISES FOR REFLECTING ON TUTORING SITUATIONS  72
EXERCISE 5A  Reflecting on Writers' Concerns  72
EXERCISE 5B  Reflecting on Your Own Writing Concerns  73
EXERCISE 5C  Reflecting on Tutoring Techniques  73
EXERCISE 5D  Learning from Scholarly Articles  73
EXERCISE 5E  Learning from Students  73

**6  Tutoring in a Digital Age  74**

Online Tutoring  74
  Synchronous Tutoring  75
  Asynchronous Tutoring  76
  ■ Stock Response for Constructing Paragraphs  79
Online Writing Resources  81
  Online Writing Labs  81
  Online Writing Guides and Handbooks  81
  Online Videos  82
Helping Writers Evaluate Online Sources  82

EXERCISES FOR TUTORING IN A DIGITAL AGE  85
EXERCISE 6A  Developing Advice Templates  85
  ■ Standardized Template  86
EXERCISE 6B  The Challenges of Online Tutoring  85
EXERCISE 6C  Creating Stock Responses  85

**7  Helping Writers across the Curriculum  87**

Research Papers  87
Lab Reports and Scientific Papers  88
Argument or Position Papers  90
Literature Papers  90
Book, Film, and Play Reviews  91

PowerPoint Presentations   92

Résumés (Traditional)   93

Résumés (Scannable)   95

Cover Letters   96

Essays of Application   97

## 8   Coping with Different Tutoring Situations   99

The Writer Who Comes at the Last Minute   99

The Unresponsive Writer   100

The Antagonistic Writer   101

The Writer Who Selects an Inappropriate Topic
or Uses Offensive Language   102

The Writer Who Plagiarizes   102

The Writer with the "Perfect" Paper   105

The Writer with the Long Paper   105

**EXERCISES FOR COPING WITH DIFFERENT
TUTORING SITUATIONS 106**

EXERCISE 8A    Role-Playing Different Tutoring Situations   106

EXERCISE 8B    Reflecting on Different Tutoring Situations   110

## 9   Summing It All Up   111

**EXERCISES FOR DEVELOPING YOUR
PHILOSOPHY OF TUTORING**   112

EXERCISE 9A    Reflecting on Your Tutoring   112

EXERCISE 9B    Creating a Metaphor for Tutoring   113

APPENDIX A   Tutors Ask . . .   115

APPENDIX B   Tutors Talk: Evaluating What They Say   119

APPENDIX C   Presenting at a Conference   121

APPENDIX D   Outside Tutoring and Editing Jobs   124

Index   127

# 1

# The Writing Center as a Workplace

Tutoring writing students can be an exciting, enjoyable, and rewarding experience. You may be tutoring in a writing center, for a company, or on your own; in each case, you become part of a long history of people involved in this profession.

Being engaged in a professional activity has ethical implications for your behavior with writers; it influences how you conduct yourself as part of a group, how you relate to other tutors, and how you function as a representative of the writing center. Tutoring involves both responsibility and trust; therefore, you are encouraged to observe certain principles of conduct in your relationships with writers, other tutors, and teachers. To make apprehensive writers feel more comfortable, writing centers tend deliberately to project an inviting, relaxed atmosphere. Tutors reflect this ambience through their casual friendliness.

Occasionally, however, tutors may be tempted to behave in too casual a manner, forgetting for the moment the professional nature of tutoring. Because you may begin tutoring at the same time that you start reading this book, you should be familiar with the following principles at the outset.

## Professionalism toward the Writer

- When writers arrive, be pleasant and courteous. They may feel uneasy about showing their writing to a tutor, and those coming in for the first time may be unsure about writing center procedures. Make sure everyone feels welcome. Although you may intend it as a gesture of goodwill, being flippant or sarcastic may put some writers off. If you are working online with a writer, be aware of your tone. It may take a few extra moments to type out a nice welcome message, but setting a friendly tone for the entire online session is important.

- Greet each writer cheerfully and indicate that you are ready to begin work, even if you are tired or under stress from school or job responsibilities. Especially in the reception area, be careful about discussing

**1**

whose turn it is to tutor or making comments like, "Who wants to work with this one?" Such behavior might make a writer wonder what kind of help a grudging tutor will deliver.

- It is fine to be relaxed at the writing center, but excessively informal behavior—conducting personal conversations with other tutors or casually touching students, for instance—may offend writers, especially those with different cultural backgrounds. Similarly, when working online with a writer, do not assume that he or she is aware of texting shorthand like *LOL* or *BTW*. Such slang can be confusing and off-putting. However, if the writer first engages in texting shorthand, and it is within the guidelines of your writing center, feel free to continue in this tone, as it may make the writer more comfortable.

- Avoid negative comments about a writer's topic. The writer may have personal reasons for choosing a particular poem to explicate or something controversial to explore. Even if the writer does not seem happy about the topic, it is best to be positive from the outset: this will set the tone for the rest of the tutoring session.

- Honor the confidentiality of the tutoring relationship: Don't comment on or discuss writers or their papers with teachers or in front of other people. Idle comments—whether praise or complaints—about writers may get back to them. Such comments may also be overheard by other clients who visit the writing center, making them wonder what will be said about them when they leave. If you need advice or want to vent about a difficult tutoring session, seek out your director or another administrator privately.

## Professionalism toward Other Tutors

- Being professional means reporting for work on time or calling and/or e-mailing beforehand if something prevents you from being there as scheduled. Like you, other tutors juggle class, work, and home schedules. Your co-workers must pick up the slack when you do not manage your time effectively.

- Be aware that carelessness or delinquency on your part makes someone else's job more difficult. Make sure that you follow all the procedures and rules of your workplace, from putting materials away to filling out time cards to filing tutoring reports.

- Tutors and writers often work in close quarters, so keep your voice down. Tidy up your workstation before you leave so that it will be ready for the next tutor.

- If you have a few idle moments, take the initiative to engage in a helpful task. Beyond tutoring, there are often odd jobs, ranging from filing papers to making coffee, that need to be done in order to keep the writing center running smoothly.

## Professionalism toward Teachers

- Teachers need to be sure that they are evaluating a writer's own work; therefore, never write any part of a student's paper. Instead, use guiding questions and comments to help writers recognize their difficulties and come up with their own solutions for revising their texts. Though you may sometimes recast a sentence or two as an example, be careful about how much of the writer's work you revise. If you need more examples, make up some or find exercises in a grammar handbook or online writing resource. If you find yourself tempted to revise too much of a writer's work, put your pencil down or walk away from your computer.

- As a tutor, you will hear writers' comments about instructors, assignments, and grading policies. Some comments may be negative, and some writers may press you to agree. Be careful, however, never to comment negatively to students about a teacher's methods, assignments, personality, or grading policies. Recognize that you cannot know everything that transpires in a classroom; even if you think you do, it is unprofessional to pass judgment. In addition, keep in mind that writers are relating their impressions or interpretations, and these may be incomplete or even inaccurate. More often than not, there are valid explanations for what may appear to be a problem. What seems to be an imperfect description of an assignment, for example, may be based on previous assignments or may have been elaborated on in class. If you cannot understand an assignment or a grading policy, send the writer back to the teacher for clarification.

- Some writers may ask a question like "Is this paper good enough for a B?" and others may pressure you to suggest a grade. Accommodating such a request is asking for trouble. Assigning grades is a subjective matter that requires experience and training, and it is the teacher's job, not the tutor's. Again, you cannot know all that has been discussed or explained in class, in e-mails, or in assignment descriptions. Furthermore, even if a paper seems well written, it is wise to be judicious with your praise. A writer may interpret your comment that "this is a good paper" to mean that it deserves an A. Suggesting or insinuating a grade can cause significant difficulties. A writer's receiving a lower grade than you mentioned could create conflicts among the teacher, the student, and the writing center. A writer who receives a higher grade than predicted by a tutor might come to doubt the writing center's judgment.

- Never criticize the grade that a teacher has given a paper. Just as suggesting a grade for a paper can lead to trouble, so too can acknowledging

to the student that you disagree with a grade. Sometimes a student who is unhappy about a grade will actively seek support from a tutor for his or her dissatisfaction. Even if you agree with the student, do not say so. Recognize that you may not be aware of all the factors that led to the grade. Students should first try to resolve concerns about grades with the teacher, and then, if necessary, talk with other appropriate people.

As a tutor, you will help many friendly, hardworking, conscientious students become better writers. However, as in any professional setting, you may occasionally encounter some difficult situations. Whether it is the fifth paper on electronic voting you have seen, a consistently late co-worker, a writer who wants you to predict a grade, or a teacher who wants to discuss his student's paper, we hope that these principles will help you conduct yourself in a professional manner.

To the writers you encounter, you represent the writing center. They judge the writing center not only by the competency of your tutoring but also by the attitudes, courtesy, and respect you display toward them and your co-workers.

## Exercises for Getting Started

### EXERCISE 1A   Keeping a Personal Tutoring Journal

A journal provides a way to record your progress as a tutor, to give voice to your observations, and even to write your way toward solutions to problems that you may encounter in the writing center. Write in your journal at least once a week about your tutoring experiences—the successes, the problems, the questions—and your thoughts about them. Write about your observations regarding the writing process and working with particular kinds of students or assignments. Record your reactions to readings, writing assignments, or topics covered in tutor meetings or other classes involving writing.

You may keep this journal for your own use, or you may write it as a dialogue journal (in effect, an exchange of friendly letters or e-mails). Arrange for an audience—perhaps your director—to respond to your writings on a regular basis, probably weekly. Or you might exchange journals regularly with another tutor and respond to one another's comments; in this way, you can learn with and from each other. Do remember, however, to keep each other's writings confidential, and share them only if you get permission first. Also, make sure you select an appropriate venue for your journal. For example, a blog may not be the best forum for your personal reflections on tutoring, especially because you may be commenting on your frustrations with particular tutoring situations.

Because journal conversation is just that—conversation—you should feel free to use informal language.

### EXERCISE 1B  Participating in Discussion Forums

Sometimes groups of tutors—a class or even the entire writing center staff—find Web-based forums such as e-mail discussion lists, real-time discussions, wikis, Facebook, or blogs helpful to explore issues and questions that arise as they tutor or to continue discussions about tutoring and writing begun in class or in meetings. Additionally, on a regular basis (perhaps weekly), the instructor, director, or designated tutors may raise particular questions or issues. Everyone in the group can then respond and contribute to the conversation.

### EXERCISE 1C  Learning about Writing Center History

Learn more about your writing center's history. Many centers have existed for years. As you and other tutors assist writers now, you may not realize that you are part of a history, one that can be interesting to explore. Interview someone knowledgeable about the writing center's background, perhaps your director. When and why was it established? Has its mission changed over time? If so, how and why? In what other ways has it changed? (In the number and kinds of tutors? In services? In the number and kinds of writers served? In location? In the influences of technology?) What stories can this person share about earlier days? Ask your director if this person can address other tutors, perhaps in a meeting, a tutor training class, or an online forum. Consider also inviting some former tutors to talk about their experiences in the writing center. If your writing center or school publishes a newsletter or newspaper, consider submitting an article about your writing center based on your research.

# 2
# The Writing Process

How does your day begin at the writing center? Do you exchange greetings with other tutors, pour yourself a cup of coffee, and check your schedule? Do you unlock the door to your one-room office and post a sign-up sheet on the door? Or do you settle in at your desk, log on to the Internet, and download tutoring requests or begin a chat session? Writing centers differ widely in their facilities, procedures, and resources; however, you will find one constant from center to center: students seeking help as they work through different stages of the writing process. Let us meet a few:

- As he takes a seat, Tom waves several sheets of paper. "Here are my notes," he tells the tutor. "I did a collecting project in my folklore class, and now I have to write a paper about what I learned from doing the project. I have a bunch of ideas, but I'm not sure which ones would be good to use."

- Keisha initiates an online chat session to get help on her lab report. She pastes a description of her assignment into the chat box and types, "This is the first lab report of the semester. It's for my biology course, and I've never written one before. Am I off to a good start? I don't really understand what to do."

- Rummaging through her book bag, Maria pulls out a draft of an essay for a graduate school application. She describes it as "boring" and asks, "What can I do to make it more interesting for the people who read these essays?"

- Chu opens her laptop and pulls up her paper: summaries of several articles on the role of psychology in education. "I just want to make sure my paper is right," she explains. As she fishes a piece of paper out of her notebook, she adds, "We got this handout explaining summaries, and it's got a list of mistakes you can make in summaries. I know I didn't plagiarize, but I'm not sure about some of the others."

- Miguel submits his paper electronically to the writing center. He explains, "I did this paper for my business writing class. I think the

© 1973 United Features Syndicate, Inc.

paper's okay, but I always have trouble with things like commas and semicolons. Please edit my punctuation."

Each of these writers is at a different stage in the writing process. Before we look at the specific stages, let us take a broader look at the writing process. The work of composition researchers and theorists like Janet Emig, Sondra Perl, Linda Flower, Peter Elbow, and Donald Murray shows that the linear model of prewriting, writing, and revising is inadequate. We now recognize that writing is a process of discovery — of exploring, testing, and refining ideas, then figuring out the most effective way to communicate those ideas to an audience. As Peter Elbow explains, "Meaning is not what you start out with but what you end up with."[1] Writing is also recursive, which means that, as writers, we continually return to earlier portions of a draft, generating new ideas and deleting others, writing and rewriting in order to move forward with the paper. Some writers make global revisions — major changes in content, focus, organization, point of view, or tone — after completing a first draft. Others follow the example of a student writer who recently explained, "As soon as I start writing even just a few words, I start revising." Throughout this backward and forward movement, we struggle to observe the constraints of writing conventions. Simultaneously, we go about the complicated tasks of creating meaning and adapting the needs of the reader to our goals as writers. Look at the following list of writing experiences to see if you can identify with any of them. Have you ever

- written and rewritten for hours, only to find that you have two useful sentences from many pages?
- written a section midway through your paper that forced you to make significant changes in what you had written in previous pages?
- carefully made a list of the important points to include in a paper and then discovered partway through writing that two of the points were unnecessary?
- struggled to fit a sentence at the end of a paragraph and then discovered that it fit perfectly at the beginning?
- spent an evening writing and rewriting an introduction, unable to get it together, and then had the perfect introduction spring forth when you began writing the next day?

---

[1]Peter Elbow. *Writing without Teachers*. New York: Oxford University Press, 1975, 15.

- returned again and again to your thesis, changing it little by little as you worked out the argument in your essay?
- tried to write a letter of complaint and found that you had to write the angry, "no holds barred" letter before you could write the more controlled, reasonable one?

As you can see, we cannot outline the writing process as we can a recipe in a cookbook. No single set of simple steps is guaranteed to produce an effective paper every time. As William Zinsser notes, "Writing is no respecter of blueprints—it's too subjective a process, too full of surprises."[2] Nonetheless, writing teachers and books on writing offer a variety of helpful descriptions of the process. These descriptions enable us to think of writing as something that happens in stages and to talk about it more easily with other writers. Most importantly, at each stage we can discuss a variety of workable strategies with the writers seeking our help, strategies that fit with our goal as writing tutors: *to make the people we work with better writers by facilitating changes in the way in which they view and produce writing.*

The following pages offer a general guide to the stages of the writing process. Each stage includes a brief discussion about one of the writers introduced at the beginning of this chapter and how his or her writing concerns fit into that particular stage. In Chapter 4, you will find suggestions for helping writers through each stage of the writing process.

## A General Guide to Stages of the Writing Process

### PREWRITING

The prewriting stage consists of invention and planning. To generate ideas, we may use such strategies as freewriting, brainstorming, researching, or observing. Then, we must plan our writing, focusing our thoughts and ideas and deciding how we should organize them. As an important part of prewriting, we also consider the audience we are addressing and our purpose for addressing them. Asking ourselves "To whom am I writing?" (the audience) and "Why?" (the purpose) helps us to determine what information to include and how to present it. We can then organize our ideas, at least loosely, into some workable plan.

Tom, who is unsure of what to do with the notes from his folklore project, is at the prewriting stage. First, he needs to identify and assess his audience and his purpose. Then, he needs to see how the information that he has gathered fits with that purpose. Does he have enough information to at least start a draft? How can he effectively arrange his material?

And what about Keisha's online request for writing help? If you recall, she seemed to be confused about how to begin her lab report and overwhelmed by the idea of producing the first assignment for the course. To

---

[2]William Zinsser. *On Writing Well: An Informal Guide to Writing Nonfiction.* 6th ed. New York: HarperCollins, 1998, 63.

get started, Keisha should explore writing conventions related to science, particularly what is expected in a lab report. Then, she needs to understand the writing process as a series of smaller, manageable tasks rather than one huge, seemingly impossible undertaking. As she moves through the prewriting stage, she will also take into account her audience and purpose while organizing the findings from her research and experiments.

## WRITING

In the writing stage, we get our ideas down on paper in an initial draft. Most people do their writing somewhere private, but some writers might find it helpful to draft a portion of a paper, like the introduction, in the writing center where they can get some immediate feedback.

Consider again Tom's folklore paper. If his ideas for the paper are adequate, he might rough out an organizational strategy and begin drafting the introduction during the tutoring session, discussing his plans and thoughts at appropriate points.

## REVISING AND EDITING

Revision consists of two stages: global revision—in which we improve the "big picture" of our papers by looking at issues like content, organization, and tone—and sentence-level revision and editing—in which we attend to the finer points of our writing by strengthening and clarifying sentences and correcting errors in grammar, punctuation, and mechanics.

**Global revision.** When making global revisions, we think big. We ask questions like "Will my audience be able to follow and understand what I've written?" "How do I come across to my audience?" "Have I included enough information?" In answering these questions, we often realize that major changes in content, focus, organization, point of view, and tone are necessary. Some students resist this stage, bringing their first draft of a paper to the writing center with the belief that it is their last.

Maria, the graduate school applicant, needs help making global revisions. She has a draft but wants to make it more interesting to the reader. To do that, she needs to first identify her audience and purpose for writing. Who will be reading her essay? Why is she writing to them, and what will they be looking for? She can then consider what kinds of changes to make in her essay and perhaps rearrange, add, or delete sections in order to make her writing more effective.

With her summary of articles on the role of psychology in education, Chu is most likely at the revising stage as well. Her teacher's list, "Properties of a Poorly Written Summary," includes being verbose, offering inadequate or incomplete information, plagiarizing, adding useless material, and being too subjective. As she and the tutor read through her paper, they will be able to determine what she may need to revise.

**Sentence-level revision and editing.**   When making sentence-level revisions, we try to improve individual sentences by cutting excessive words, clarifying confusing or improperly constructed sentences, or trying to find more exact words for the ideas that we want to express. In the editing stage, we correct errors in grammar, punctuation, and mechanics.

After revising and editing, we proofread, looking for typographical errors, omitted words, and other mistakes that we might have missed earlier. Remember Miguel, who asked his online tutor to "edit the punctuation" in the paper for his business writing class? He needs help with the editing stage, but rather than make the changes for him, the tutor should identify Miguel's error patterns, model one or two corrections, and encourage him to look for the same errors elsewhere in his paper. An aside: The tutor may likely notice that Miguel needs to make some global revisions or sentence-

---

### Stages of the Writing Process

**PREWRITING**

| | |
|---|---|
| Freewriting | Focusing on thoughts and ideas |
| Brainstorming | Considering audience |
| Researching | Organizing loosely |
| Observing | Creating a workable plan |

**WRITING**

Creating initial draft

**REVISING AND EDITING (USUALLY IN MULTIPLE DRAFTS)**

- *Global Revision:* Improving content, organization, tone
- *Sentence-Level Revision:* Strengthening and clarifying
- *Editing:* Correcting errors in grammar, punctuation, and mechanics
- *Proofreading:* Looking for typographical errors, omitted words, and other mistakes

level revisions that involve more than punctuation, for writers often use catchphrases like *editing* or *proofreading* when asking for help with more general revision.

## Exercises for Exploring the Writing Process

The following exercises allow you to explore the writing process in several different ways: by considering how others describe the stages, by looking at how writing is taught at your school, by examining the language people use to talk about writing, and by taking a close look at your own writing process. You may do the exercises independently or in conjunction with a training course, and they can provide good starting points for group discussion.

### EXERCISE 2A   Comparing Writing Guides and Handbooks

Choose four different guides or handbooks on writing. Make a list of the terms that they use to describe the stages of the writing process, and compare and contrast the ways in which they describe the stages. Set up the comparisons in the way that works best for you. You may want to sketch out your own informal chart.

### EXERCISE 2B   Teaching Writing

How are writing and the writing process taught at your school? To answer this question, you should explore a variety of resources. The following list offers suggestions for questions to answer and ways to go about this task. You may wish to do this exercise in small groups, working together or dividing up the tasks.

1. *Courses.* What writing courses are offered? Are they face-to-face, online, or hybrid courses? Are there courses for second language writers, those students for whom English is a second language (ESL)? For basic writers or those not ready to take a standard composition course? For honors students? Are there classes in intermediate or advanced composition? Are there courses in business or technical writing or other specialized areas? Are some courses sequential?

2. *Course descriptions.* Are there written descriptions of these courses? Often, school catalogs include short descriptions, but some writing programs offer more expanded explanations of the purpose and goals for each course. How does one course differ from another?

3. *Textbooks.* What textbooks (guides to writing, handbooks, readers, style manuals, online materials) are being used at your school? Your writing center or writing program office may have copies that you can examine, or you might check the shelves in the school bookstore or locate them online. Look through these texts. How are they organized?

4. *Syllabi.* Does each writing course have a standard syllabus, or do teachers write their own? Check to see if your writing center or writing program office has a file of sample syllabi or if sample syllabi are posted online. If not, you might ask several teachers for copies. What kinds of assignments are included? Do they follow a particular sequence? How do instructors incorporate textbook or online material into their courses?

5. *Assignments.* How are assignments given? Are they taken from the textbooks? Do teachers provide descriptions explaining the assignments? To answer these questions, you might poll several instructors, or you might check to see if there is a file of typical assignments.

6. *Technology.* Is technology a part of writing classes? How is it incorporated in writing instruction? Do some or all classes meet online or in a smart classroom or computer lab? How—and how widely—do writing classes use the lab? Do any classes use Web environments like Blackboard, CompClass, Second Life, or open-source forums? Do classroom lectures and/or assignments include PowerPoint presentations, Web pages, or other online formats, such as Wikis, podcasts, or Twitter?

7. *Competency exams.* Do any of the writing courses at your school use competency exams? Are they given during the course or at the end? What format(s) do they follow? What aspects of writing do they stress? If your writing center does not have a file of competency tests, try to get copies of old tests or practice tests from instructors. You may also want to talk to instructors about how and why they use them.

8. *Writing-intensive courses.* Are there writing-intensive courses, perhaps as part of a writing across the curriculum (WAC) or a writing in the disciplines (WID) program? What defines these classes as being writing intensive? Are there guidelines for these classes? What are they like? What, if any, writing textbooks (perhaps a handbook or style manual) do they use?

9. *Portfolios.* Do students put together portfolios of their work in any class, perhaps for evaluation? How many and what kind of materials are included in the portfolio? Are they sequential or themed?

### EXERCISE 2C    Talking about the Writing Process

When students meet with tutors, they use a variety of terms to discuss their writing. Many students echo their teachers and the ways that writing is discussed in their classes.

The following is a list of common writing terms with which you should be familiar. Define the ones that you already know, and then use textbooks and other resources from your school's writing program or writing center to define the rest.

| | | |
|---|---|---|
| Audience | Format | Rubric |
| Brainstorming | Freewriting | Subject-verb agreement |
| Coherence | Heuristics | |
| Comma splices | Invention | Thesis |
| Composing process | Mechanics | Tone |
| Emphasis | Organization | Topic sentence |
| Final draft | Point of view | Voice |
| First draft | Revision | |

## EXERCISE 2D   Talking about the Writing Process at Your School

The preceding list of terms is by no means exhaustive, for we commonly use many other terms as we discuss writing. Make a list of additional terms (with definitions) that might be used to discuss writing in your writing center. Your school may base its writing instruction on a particular textbook or approach to teaching writing, and you will need to be familiar with terms particular to that book or approach. Tutors at the University of Maryland Writing Center, for example, would add several terms from classical rhetoric—like *ethos*, *logos*, and *pathos*—because many writing teachers at that school use these terms in their classes.

## Exercises for Reflecting on Your Writing Process

In order to work with writers, you will need to become familiar with a variety of writing strategies. One way to begin is to start where you are an expert: with your own writing process and writing history. Because you have been writing for many years, you have some ideas about what works (and what does not work) for you when you confront a writing task. But you have probably never taken a formal look at what you actually do from the moment you are given an assignment to the moment you hand it in.

Shoe–New Business Macnelly. Distributed by King Features Syndicate.

Exercise 2E asks you to write a paper in which you reflect on your writing process; Exercises 2F and 2G build on that assignment by asking you to discuss and reflect on your experiences.

### EXERCISE 2E   Reflecting on Writing

Choose one of the following topics, and write an essay of three to five pages. Go to writing center tutors for assistance at least twice as you work on your paper. You may go at any time during your writing process, but work with two different tutors.

**Topic 1: How I write.**   We all go about writing in idiosyncratic ways. We find what works for us and what does not; then, we try to capitalize on the former and minimize the latter. Your task in this paper is to examine and discuss your own writing process. You may describe how you go about writing in general, or you may focus on a piece of writing that you have completed recently. As you compose, keep in mind that writing should delight as well as instruct. Consider other tutors to be your audience, and use the following questions as a guide:

- When you are confronted with a writing task, how do you approach it? Do you spend days fretting about it? Immediately jot down ideas and then start playing with them? Perform an online search of relevant terms to get an idea of what's out there? Think for days and then produce a first draft in one sitting?

- How do you go about producing a draft? Do you carefully assemble specific materials—like three sharp pencils and a legal-size pad? Don comfortable clothes—perhaps a favorite sweatshirt—and sit down at your laptop? Create an introduction that "will suffice" and then rework it later? Write, pace the floor a bit, write again, pace again?

- Do you write with the advice of a particular person—maybe a former teacher—echoing in your mind as you compose?

- When do you begin to consciously consider your audience? From the outset? As you revise your first draft? Do you seek advice as you write? Do you talk to others about your ideas and perhaps about how you organize them? Do you read to or show people drafts or parts of drafts? What kinds of feedback do you look for? When others give you suggestions, how do you factor them in?

- How do you feel when you have completed a paper? Are you simply glad that it is done? Are you convinced that one more pass would produce a better paper?

**Topic 2: Writing autobiography.**   How did you become the writer you are now? In this paper, your task is to explore your history as a writer. Consider the following questions as you plan your paper. Though you need not answer all of the questions, use them as prompts to stimulate your thinking about your engagement with writing and about your writing process.

- When did you begin writing? How old were you, what did you write about, and how did you go about it? How have innovations in technology changed the way you think or approach writing tasks?

- As you matured, how did your writing and the ways you went about it change? Did anyone or anything influence your writing? If so, who or what, and how?

- What kinds of writing do you do now or have you done? Have you written a diary or journal? Letters to a pen pal or family members? E-mail, blogs, Twitter entries, Facebook postings, or on other online venues?

- What are your favorite and least favorite aspects of the writing process? What could you do to make your writing more effective?

- How do you see writing fitting into your life, both formally and informally, in the future?

### EXERCISE 2F   Sharing Your Writing Process

The previous exercise is an ideal departure point for group discussion. If possible, meet with a group of tutors and read your papers aloud, or post your papers online for others to read and comment on. Compare and contrast the different ways you each go about a writing task. You will probably find a variety of approaches among members of your group. As others share, take notes—first, to pick up some hints for making your own process more efficient and, second, to begin compiling suggestions that you might offer students who seek your help.

### EXERCISE 2G    Reflecting on Being Tutored

When your group has finished Exercise 2F and discussed your writing processes, shift your attention to the two tutoring sessions that you each had in Exercise 2E. One of the best ways to discover how people feel about an experience is to put yourself in their shoes. You are learning to be a tutor, but you have just had the experience of sitting in the other chair—that of the writer being tutored—twice. Take five minutes to jot down your responses to the following questions, and then discuss your answers.

- How did you feel about getting help from a tutor?
- What did the tutor do or suggest that you found helpful, in terms of both completing your assignment and making you feel more comfortable about getting help with your writing?
- Conversely, what, if anything, did the tutor do or say that confused you or made you feel uncomfortable?

# 3

# Inside the Tutoring Session

The following strategies for working with writers in tutoring sessions are equally appropriate and applicable for face-to-face or synchronous tutoring scenarios. When referring to online tutoring, we use the terms *synchronous* and *asynchronous*. Synchronous tutoring is in real time; it usually takes place in chat forums and the writer and tutor have a real-time conversation online. Asynchronous tutoring is not conducted in real time; the writer submits a question or draft for review, and the tutor responds within an allotted time. When a strategy unique to the asynchronous tutoring session is called for, we have included it here.

## Getting Started

It is not by accident that many writing centers appear welcoming and friendly. To make writers feel more comfortable, centers are often furnished with plants, bright posters, comfortable chairs, and tables instead of desks. Online writing centers do their part by offering attractive Web pages with helpful, user-friendly language and links and by having a presence in forums such as Facebook or Second Life. Whether you meet writers face-to-face or online, you should try to put them at ease. A casual but interested greeting and a smile—or an emoticon—can immediately make them less apprehensive about the prospect of sharing their writing. At a face-to-face writing center, be alert for those reluctant writers who hover about the doorway, unsure of what to do. Invite them in with a cheerful "Can I help you?" In an online writing center, especially in asynchronous sessions, look for those "quiet" writers who submit their papers without any information about what kind of help they are looking for. Write an encouraging note and ask for a more detailed description of the assignment or what they struggled with as they wrote their papers.

The following are tips to help establish rapport at the beginning of the tutoring session:

- **Introduce yourself.** Smile and ask the writer his or her name. Once you have settled into a comfortable place for the two of you to work, ask about the assignment and how it is going. If you have worked with the writer before, ask how the last assignment went. The exchange of pleasantries at the beginning of a session helps put the writer at ease and gets the session off to a good start.

    In an online environment, you may be able to access records of the writer's previous submissions that you can then ask about or refer to. Even if the writer cannot respond to you immediately, he or she will be more inclined to provide additional information with the next submission.

- **Sit side-by-side.** Such a setup is the best arrangement for tutoring; it suggests that you are an ally, not an authoritarian figure who dispenses advice from behind a desk. Sitting side-by-side allows you and the writer to look at the work in progress together, but you can still position your chairs to look at one another as you converse if you like. If you do use a desk, have the writer sit at the side of it rather than across from you.

    Just as this arrangement conveys a nonverbal message, be aware that your body language and clothing also express unspoken messages. Sit in a relaxed and comfortable manner, and demonstrate interest in the writer's words by leaning forward and making eye contact. Dress casually but appropriately for work.

- **Give the student control of the paper.** Keep the paper in front of the student as much as possible. As a general rule, if you are working at a computer, let the writer control the keyboard and monitor. Positioning the writer in front of the paper or computer serves to remind him or her (and sometimes the tutor) that the writing is that of the student. Having the writer at the keyboard also ensures that you serve as the audience: two people cannot type simultaneously on the same keyboard.

    In an online environment, resist the urge to correct and edit mistakes as you read. Instead, indicate patterns of error and ask leading, probing questions that will require the writer to take control of the paper when he or she reads and considers your advice.

- **Keep resources and tools nearby.** Have scrap paper and pencils handy. Though it is generally a good idea to let the student do most of the writing, you may occasionally wish to demonstrate a point in writing, or it may be more expedient for you to make notes for the writer. It is wise for online tutors to keep a list of resource links in a Favorites folder so that they can be embedded in the comments. As you work, have print and online resources—like a dictionary, thesaurus, and grammar handbook—readily available.

## Setting the Agenda

During the first several minutes, you and the writer will be setting at least a tentative agenda for the tutoring session, and the best way to do that is to talk or chat. Conversation not only establishes rapport but also engages the writer in the session immediately. In addition, it allows you to learn fairly quickly about the assignment and the writer and about his or her approaches to and concerns about the task at hand, as well as writing in general—all necessary information to determine how to spend your time together most effectively and efficiently.

As a new tutor, you may feel uncomfortable with an extended conversation. You may think that looking at the assignment description and the student's paper gives you something concrete to do, and you may worry that a conversation could go in unpredictable directions. Recognize, however, that this initial conversation allows you not only to establish a comfortable acquaintance but also to gather information and assess the writer's needs. As an intelligent, interested, and friendly audience, you will find it relatively easy to talk and learn more about the assignment and the writer. Then, you can put your newly acquired tutoring skills to work more easily and productively.

How to begin? Quite simply, ask questions and show interest.

- "What can I help you with?"
- "What assignment are you working on?"
- "Who is your audience?"
- "What are you writing about?"
- "What a fascinating topic! Why did you choose it?"
- "What approach did you take?"
- "Can you tell me (briefly) how you set up your argument?"

As the writer answers, seek clarification with follow-up questions that encourage him or her to talk more. This time spent talking means that when you finally look at the paper, you will be able to match the writer's goals more adequately with what actually appears in the paper and more readily offer suggestions to make the writing more effective.

If the assignment is unfamiliar, read through the description quickly to be sure the writer has not forgotten or misunderstood any details, but not so quickly that you miss any important information. (Even if the assignment is a common one, it is probably a good idea to glance through the description in case the instructor has made any changes.) Rather than have the writer wait for the session to begin, engage him or her with comments or questions as you read, like "I see you have to..." or "What did you choose for...?" Asking writers to articulate the assignment—and their approach to it—often allows you to uncover any misunderstandings or apprehensions that they may have. A writer will often respond to your question "What can I help you with?" quite specifically, which simplifies setting an agenda

Reprinted by permission of the artist.

for the session. The writer may explain, for example, that "the introduction just doesn't seem to do what I want it to" or "the paper reads too much like a list." However, be aware that some writers will simply ask for help with "proofreading," "editing," or "grammar," using these terms to cover any aspect of revising from major reorganizing to eliminating wordiness to correcting punctuation.

How you and the writer ultimately spend your time depends on the following factors:

- Where is the writer in the composing process?
- What are the constraints imposed by the assignment itself—the inherent limitations and those imposed by the teacher (such as length, number of resources to be used, and so on)?
- How much time remains before the paper is due?
- How willing is the writer to work with the tutor in order to improve the paper?

When working asynchronously, you must still set the agenda, even if it is just to ensure that you use your time appropriately. Carefully consider the above questions and try to prioritize the areas that need the most attention.

Another important factor is the length of time allotted for each tutoring session. Most writing centers allow an hour or less for each session. Probably no session should last more than an hour. If it does, chances are the writer will be overwhelmed by suggestions or the tutor may end up doing too much of the work for the writer. For online asynchronous sessions, time is also a factor. Asynchronous sessions tend to take much longer than face-to-face or synchronous sessions because, unless you have audio software, you must type out your responses. Some online writing centers simply ask that you keep your advising session to an hour or so.

If you and the writer do not jointly agree on the focus of the session at the outset, then determine what can be realistically accomplished in the time that you have, given the writer's needs. For example, some writers expect a tutor to review every page of a long paper, which is just not possible in a short time. In such a case, suggest working on a particularly troublesome section; ask the writer to identify the section of the paper giving him or her the most difficulty. You can also explain that sentence-level problems in early pages will likely recur in later pages; you can then offer suggestions for improvement on a page or two that the writer may apply to subsequent pages. Depending on the circumstances, offer options and recommend what you think are realistic goals for the session.

As you talk with the writer and look through the assignment and essay, make a list of concerns and items, either on paper or in conversation, that should or could be covered. Ultimately, this list should be understandable to both you and the writer. But how do you decide what to cover in the session? First, prioritize the list; then take into account the writer's willingness (or ability) to spend time and still meet the due date (or, on rare occasions, request an extension). Both of you can then determine what to cover in this session. Remember that it is better to cover larger, more global issues like content and organization before dealing with matters like sentence structure and surface errors. Perhaps you can factor in scheduling subsequent sessions if the list is long. Or the writer may prefer simply to concentrate on certain aspects this time and on others at another time. She or he may recognize the need to work with a tutor earlier in the writing process for future assignments.

Sometimes, a writer lacks sufficient time to truly benefit from the tutor's suggestions. There may be problems with the content or organization, for example, but the writer may only have time to correct sentence-level errors. When you encounter such a situation, explain to the writer that you cannot deal with all aspects of the paper that may need attention but will focus on the most expedient ones. Nonetheless, it is important to point out the other problem areas, and maybe some potential resources, so that the writer is aware of them as he or she writes future papers.

## Three Effective, Powerful Tools

As a tutor, you have three powerful tools at your disposal:

- Active listening
- Facilitating by responding as a reader
- Silence and wait time to allow a writer time to think

Used in combination, these tools can help you to learn and understand better what students' concerns or problems with writing may be. You can use them to induce writers to think more clearly and specifically about their audience, their purpose, their writing plan, or what they have already written. These tools also provide an excellent means of getting feedback to determine how well writers understand the suggestions or advice that you have given them.

## ACTIVE LISTENING

After exchanging pleasantries and settling down at a table, Dwight and his tutor, Kristen, begin their session. As you follow their conversation, pay particular attention to Kristen's responses to Dwight's comments and concerns.

*Kristen:* So, tell me what you're working on. What's your assignment, and what can I do to help?

*Dwight:* I'm taking this speech course on gender and communication. For our final paper, we're supposed to take five rituals connected with courtship and marriage—like the engagement ring, bachelor and bachelorette parties, the father giving away the bride, the white wedding dress—and analyze them. We're supposed to relate them to some of the concepts we've been discussing all semester. And it's due next Tuesday.

*Kristen:* That sounds like a really interesting assignment, like it would be fun to do. I haven't heard of that assignment before, so I'm a little confused. Do you have to do research for it? Tell me more.

*Dwight:* No. No research. Not really. Just what we've been doing in class. I don't know. Five to seven pages! I think it's kind of hard. I can think of rituals, but there are so many. How do I choose five that are good? I don't want to do the same ones everyone else is doing. By the time Dr. Timmons looks at my paper, he might be tired of reading about engagement rings and white wedding dresses. And then I don't know how to put them into some kind of order. I could put the most significant one first, but then I'll end up probably trailing off into the least exciting one. Boring! And I have to have a coherent paper, so I need an introduction that kind of ties these five rituals together. How do I do that?

*Kristen:* What I'm hearing you say is that this assignment is really frustrating you, and you just can't get started. It sounds like you're worrying about all of it at once. Let's see if we can get some kind of handle on this. Okay. You have to select five rituals.

*Dwight:* Yes, like the ones I mentioned. But they're the obvious ones.

*Kristen:* Perhaps. But I also heard you say that you're concerned about the length of your paper. Let's start with the rituals. You have to discuss five, but earlier you mentioned four of them—engagement rings, bachelor and bachelorette parties, wedding gowns, and fathers giving brides away.

*Dwight:* Well, the *white* wedding gown. I know, but those are so obvious.

*Kristen:* Are those rituals that you think you might have something to say about? Why did you choose those?

*Dwight:* Yeah, you might be right. You don't think they're too common? Too obvious?

*Kristen:* Maybe not. I can hear that you're very concerned that they're obvious, but if you have a lot to say about each, your paper could be really good. Probably better than if you picked something you might not know much about, like bridal shower games. Tell me more about the first one you mentioned. Let's see — the engagement ring.

When Dwight talks about his assignment, he is clearly overwhelmed and frustrated. Rather than sorting the assignment into workable tasks, he worries simultaneously about the paper's content, length, organization, due date, and engaging the reader.

What Kristen demonstrates in this scenario is active listening, a skill that takes energy and concentration. Instead of dismissing Dwight's concerns, Kristen grants them validity with statements like "What I'm hearing you say is...," "It sounds like...," "And I also heard you say that...," and "I can hear that...." She feeds back what she believes to be his message.

As the session continues, Kristen *paraphrases* Dwight's list of rituals, mirroring what she heard him say earlier. This paraphrasing accomplishes two purposes: It lets Dwight know that she has heard and understood him, but it also serves as a way to check perceptions and correct any possible misunderstandings. For example, as Dwight notes, it is not just the wedding gown that is important but the fact that it is white.

Kristen also uses questions to invite Dwight to expand on or continue his thoughts. She asks, "Why did you choose those?" and urges him to elaborate by saying, "Tell me more about...." Notice that these questions are open. Rather than requiring decisive *yes* or *no* responses, they give Dwight room to continue his thoughts and to develop them.

Finally, Kristen uses *I* statements when she says "I'm a little confused" and "I can hear...." This approach places the burden of understanding on her rather than on Dwight. If she had said, "You're not explaining things clearly," Dwight might well have become defensive. Because Kristen's questions and comments are not antagonistic, Dwight is more likely to seek out and remedy the causes for her confusion rather than to justify his apprehensions.

What we can't see in this scenario is Kristen's physical engagement in the conversation — her body language. An active listener generally communicates interest and concern by posture and eye contact. Kristen is probably leaning slightly forward, with her feet on the floor, looking directly at Dwight. Her gestures of friendliness and approval, like nodding or smiling in agreement, also help to assure him that she is interested and following what he is saying.

---

### A Note about Asking Questions

Questions can help you learn more about a writer's attitudes and specific problems with writing or with particular assignments. Questions fall into two broad categories — open and closed.

An open question — like "What have you been working on in class?" or "What can I do to help?" — is broad in scope and requires more than a few words in response. Usually, an open question begins with *what, why, when,* or *how.* Responses to such questions, especially at the beginning of a tutoring session, can help you to determine the writer's attitude toward the task at hand. Asking "What can I help you with?" invites more response than "I see you're working on a definition paper." A question like "How is the class going?" may help you to learn about the writer's performance as well as his or her expectations.

A closed question is one like "Have you got a description of your assignment?" "When is your paper due?" or "Do you have some ideas for that section?" Such questions require a *yes* or *no* or a brief, limited response and yield specific information. On the other hand, the answer to a closed question like "Who is your teacher?" may tell you something about the class or assignment, especially if you have already dealt with other students from that class.

---

When working asynchronously online, tutors do not have the benefit of back-and-forth conversation. However, they can still "listen" to the writer and use language like "I can tell..." and "It seems like you..." to show that they are engaged with the writing. The writer may have provided information about the assignment or about his or her concerns with the assignment. The tutor may also glean information from the writing itself—hesitancy when addressing a certain point or a sudden insertion of passionate (but unsupported) personal opinion.

## FACILITATING

Nikki initiates a chat with an online consultant. She has the first draft of a paper for an Introduction to Poetry class and she pastes the first two paragraphs into the chat window:

> Emily Dickinson, her poetry, and her style of writing all reflect her own feelings as well as her own ultimate dreams. Her withdrawal from the world and her impassioned art were also inspired in part I think by a tragic romance. A series of tormented and often frankly erotic letters were found to prove that this unsuccessful romance had a strong impact on her emotions—enough impact to seclude her from any outside life. This paper concerns two of Emily Dickinson's poems, number 288 and number 384, which are both prime examples that reflect the dejection she was experiencing.
>
> In poem number 288, Dickinson reveals her loneliness. In line number one, she introduces herself as "Nobody," as if it is her plural name. Nobody also

*refers to someone that people do not know much about. I think the word
Nobody uses both meanings in this poem. She then asks the reader if he or
she is Nobody too.*

Nikki's paragraphs probably raise many questions for you. Looking only
at the first sentence, for example, you might wonder: What feelings are
reflected? What dreams? How does Dickinson's style reflect these? But such
questions only mirror the confusion that Nikki is experiencing at this stage
in her writing. Though it is clear that she has thought about some ideas,
she remains unfocused. She needs help with sorting through, clarifying, and
articulating those ideas.

The best way to assist Nikki is to focus on her thoughts and ideas rather
than on the paper itself. Instead of making judgments about her draft,
describe your reactions as a reader, and ask questions that invite her to further examine, explore, and clarify her ideas and approaches. By reacting as a
reader, you are facilitating—that is, assisting and making the process easier.

The following paragraphs discuss the functions that facilitative questions and comments may serve. They offer examples as well as suggestions
for applying them to Nikki's paper.

**Reacting as a reader.**    Comments like "I'm confused," "I get lost here,"
"From your introduction, I expected to read…," and "This is what this sentence or paragraph means to me. Do I have the right idea? Is that what you
meant?" simply and honestly convey your response to a paper as you read
it. They invite writers to elaborate and, in so doing, to clarify ideas for you
and for themselves.

■ *What you might write to Nikki:* "In your introduction, you say that
Dickinson's poetry reflects her feelings and dreams and her dejection about
the unhappy romance that inspired it. But when I finish that paragraph, I'm
confused. I'm not sure exactly what your paper's going to be about." Since
Nikki's introduction mentions several aspects of Dickinson's poetry and it is
unclear which one(s) her paper will focus on, *I* statements place the burden
for the confusion on you, not Nikki, and invite her to resolve it. She will
perhaps struggle to articulate her intended focus and may come to some
new realizations about that focus.

**Requesting information.**    Questions such as "Can you tell me more
about…?" can help students to clarify their thinking, consider the whole
paper or an aspect of it more critically, refocus their thoughts, or continue a
line of thinking further.

■ *What you might write to Nikki:* "Why did you choose these two
poems? Can you tell me more about them?" Of the many poems written
by Emily Dickinson, Nikki chose two to discuss. Your requests give her an
opportunity to articulate and examine the reasons for her choice. Doing so
should help her to understand more clearly what it is she wants to say about
the poems.

**Requesting clarification.**    When students' answers or writing is vague, encourage them to clarify points by asking, "What is your idea here?" "What are you thinking?" "What do you want to say?" "What do you want your reader to know in this paragraph?" "How does this idea connect with what you said before?" "What do you mean by...?" or "Tell me more about..."

To be sure you are following and understanding what a writer intends, restate the content of the message: "What I'm hearing you say is... Do I have it right?"

■ *What you might write to Nikki:* "You say Dickinson's poetry reflects her feelings. What do you mean by 'feelings'? Which feelings?" Nikki's reference to feelings is vague, so questions will lead Nikki to consider her intentions more carefully and come to a clearer understanding of what she means to say. As she responds, you could encourage her to relate her answers to the two poems by asking, "How are Dickinson's feelings reflected in the two poems you chose?"

**Developing critical awareness.**    Writers sometimes plan or write whole papers without adequately evaluating audience or purpose, and one of the best questions that you can pose is "So what?" That question, or versions of it — such as "Why does anyone [your audience] want or need to know about that?" — forces writers to think about their purpose in addressing their audience. "So what?" also makes them consider and justify other points in the paper, as do questions like "Why would that be so?" and "Can you give me an example of...?"

■ *What you might write to Nikki:* "You indicate that the word *Nobody* is important in this poem. Why would that be so?" You might ask these questions because Nikki has singled out the word *Nobody* as being significant, but she does not clearly explain why. Your questions should encourage her to justify its importance.

**Refocusing.**    To get writers to refocus or rethink their writing, it is useful to get them to relate their approach to another idea or approach, using questions like "How would someone who disagrees respond to your argument?" "How is that related to...?" or "If that's so, what would happen if...?"

■ *What you might write to Nikki:* "You mentioned Dickinson's 'withdrawal from the world.' Didn't Dickinson also have a phobia, a fear of public places? How might that relate to her 'withdrawal from the world'?" Nikki's draft is not far enough along to begin refocusing her material, but suppose that you know something about Nikki's topic — like Dickinson's phobia — an aspect that she could at least bear in mind as she re-evaluates. Your request does not demand that Nikki address this aspect in her paper; it merely alerts her to a dimension she may be unaware of and asks her to examine whether she should consider it.

**Prompting.**    To get writers to continue or follow their line of thinking further, encourage them with questions like "What happens after that?" or "If that is so, then what happens?"

■ *What you might write to Nikki:* "What words or phrases suggest to you that she was lonely? How do those words or phrases show loneliness?" As Nikki articulates her ideas about Dickinson's poetry reflecting "feelings," she will probably mention loneliness because she includes that word in her draft. Encourage her to continue thinking along those lines.

As a facilitator, you function as a sounding board or mirror, reflecting back to writers what you hear them trying to communicate. Your stance is an objective one, for your purpose is to evoke and promote writers' ideas, not to contribute your own. As you become increasingly comfortable with tutoring and better able to size up the writers with whom you work, you may feel more at ease with occasionally offering opinions about or suggestions for content, but beware: The paper must remain the responsibility of the writer.

## SILENCE AND WAIT TIME

Try this experiment. Get a watch or clock with a second hand. At the start of a minute, turn around or place the clock out of sight. When you think that a minute has elapsed, look back. How close did you come? Thirty seconds? Forty-five? Chances are you stopped a little too soon, and that is what we tend to do when we try to make ourselves wait: We jump in a little too soon.

As a tutor, you should learn when and how to pause and be silent in a tutoring session. Occasionally, writers need time to digest what has been discussed or to formulate a question. They also need time to think about a response when you pose a question. Often, tutors are tempted to quickly rephrase a question or even answer it themselves when a writer does not respond after a moment or two. If you feel this temptation, try waiting a little longer than you think you should; then wait some more. This deliberate use of wait time communicates to writers that they are expected to think and arrive at answers on their own. You might even create an excuse to get up and leave for a few minutes; go to the restroom or get a drink of water. In a synchronous session, online silence is sometimes even more difficult to bear, as the blinking cursor seems to demand an immediate response. Feel free to type "take your time" or "I have to leave the computer for a couple of minutes; I'll be right back!" to give the writer some online breathing room.

Thinking time is especially important when a new aspect of a topic arises, and writers may even need a few moments on their own to do some writing. Try initiating short breaks that allow writers five or even ten minutes to freewrite, brainstorm, or draft a section of a paper. On other occasions, you might give them time to complete an activity that relates to what you have just been discussing. You might ask them to revise a portion of their draft or correct certain problems with grammar, mechanics, or punctuation. Or they might complete a short grammar exercise. When they finish, you can review their work with them. When chatting, simply give them a set amount of time to work on a discrete task ("I'm going to give you five minutes; I'll be here when you want to resume."). Resist the urge to maintain constant online chatter; instead, give them the time and space necessary to compose their thoughts.

## WRAPPING UP A SESSION

Some sessions end gracefully when you and the writer finish addressing the writer's concerns and needs; however, not all sessions are ready to end when the allotted time is almost up. There may even be awkwardness: Another writer may be waiting for you, or you may be anxious to pack up and run to class. One good way to handle wrapping up a session is to watch the clock unobtrusively and announce when there are five to ten minutes left. You and the writer can finish what you are working on, plan the writer's next steps or next session, and answer any last questions. Another approach is to ask the writer if there is anything specific that he or she wants to cover in those last minutes; you might begin by briefly summarizing what you've worked on—or ask the writer to summarize the session—then ask if there is any other question you can answer before he or she leaves. In some writing centers, tutors complete a report form summing up what was accomplished; inviting the writer to contribute or comment on the form can also serve as a graceful way to wrap up a session. Online tutors often provide a final checklist; if working synchronously, the tutor can ask the writer to help generate the list.

# The Many Hats Tutors Wear

A tutor's role varies from session to session. With one writer, you ask question after question to help him figure out what he has to say about a scene in *Beowulf*. With the next, you explain the various ways of defining a term in a definition paper. In the midst of this session, the student vents some frustrations about being a returning student and balancing her time, so you direct her to a series of workshops for returning students. Then, a second language writer arrives. He cannot get his subjects and verbs to agree; you pull out a piece of paper and start explaining. In your tutoring, you function variously as an ally, a coach, a commentator, a collaborator, a writing "expert," a learner, and a counselor.

## THE ALLY

You are a friend who offers support to a writer coping with a difficult task—writing a paper. You are sympathetic, empathetic, and encouraging, and best of all, you are supportive and helpful. You explain things in terms that the writer can understand. You answer questions that may seem silly or stupid, but you take them seriously. You smile (in person or online: ☺). You understand. After all, didn't you just explain that you have a history paper due tomorrow, and you do not expect to get much sleep tonight either?

## THE COACH

In sports, coaches instruct players and direct team strategy. They do not actually do the work for the team, but rather they stand on the sidelines observing how the team functions, looking at what is going well and what needs improvement. Likewise, you stand on the sidelines. The work of writers needs to be their own, but by asking questions, making comments, and functioning as a reader, you encourage writers to think through problems and to find their own answers. You suggest ways of accomplishing tasks. You describe how to organize a comparison and contrast paper, clarify the rules for using a semicolon, or explain and help students implement strategies for invention.

## THE COMMENTATOR

Sports commentators give play-by-play accounts, but they also give a picture of the whole game as it progresses. Likewise, you describe process and progress in a broader context than a writer might otherwise see. As former Purdue University professor and writing lab director Muriel Harris explains, "The tutor-commentator provides perspective, makes connections to larger issues, gives students a sense of when and how they are moving forward."[1] You enable writers to see a paper as a whole by working with them to establish goals and by explaining what work lies ahead. You help them to acquire strategies and skills that will work not just for this paper but for others as well. You point out that making a correction in spelling or punctuation is not simply a matter of following a convention but rather of making their writing more accessible for a reader.

## THE COLLABORATOR

You know that writers are supposed to do all of the work themselves, but you are discussing ideas for a paper with a particularly sharp writer. She has read Kate Chopin's *The Awakening* and has focused on examining the color imagery in it. You have just read the book, so you know what she is talking about. She mentions the dinner scene, and you have an idea about the color yellow in it. Do you keep it to yourself? Probably not. More likely, the two of you discuss ideas about the imagery in a mutually engaging and even exhilarating exchange; she profits from your input and you from hers.

Such an exchange may seem like the best part of tutoring, but if you do share your ideas with writers, be wary of two potential problems. First,

---

[1]Muriel Harris. "The Roles a Tutor Plays: Effective Tutoring Techniques." *English Journal* 69.9 (1980): 62–65.

© 1987 United Features Syndicate, Inc.

writers should always be responsible for and in control of their own papers. Lazy or unsure writers may try to rely on you to produce most or all of the ideas for papers—in effect, to write the paper—which should be their own work. Conversely, the overzealous tutor may usurp papers, interjecting too many ideas and leaving writers confused, no longer in control of the paper, and perhaps less confident about their writing abilities.

## THE WRITING "EXPERT"

You may not be a writing teacher or a writing expert; nonetheless, students usually come to you assuming that you know more about writing than they do. The truth is that you probably do. Just by being a tutor, you become more knowledgeable about writing. You are an example of the adage that we learn best when we explain something to someone else.

But what do you do when you realize that you are in over your head, that you do not know how to explain a grammatical point or the options available when writing a résumé? The simple answer is to admit that you do not know and then to seek help. Check—or have the student check—a textbook, handbook, or Web site; thus, you model how one can use available resources. You can also ask another tutor, who can often be an excellent resource. Occasionally, you may need to turn the writer over to a more knowledgeable tutor. In that case, you might sit in (or read the advice if tutoring online) and learn something for the next time that you encounter a similar situation.

## THE LEARNER

This role is slightly different than the others in this list because, while it has some benefits for writers, you are the one who really gains. Students submit papers on a wide variety of topics, some of which will be partially or entirely new to you. What, for example, causes chrondomalacia, or "runner's knee," and how is it treated? How is oil extracted from shale? What does Chief Seattle say about environmental issues in his 1854 speech? What is "ghost dancing," and how did it contribute to the massacre at Wounded Knee on the South Dakota Pine Ridge reservation? As you talk with writers, you get to enjoy learning about these and other topics. Even if you are familiar with a topic, the perspective that the writer takes may help you see it in a new or different way. For example, a student's discussion of Isabella in Shakespeare's *Measure for Measure* as a kind of "typical teenager" may lead you to consider that character differently.

Knowing little or nothing about a topic often makes you a perfect audience for a paper, so writers actually gain from your lack of expertise. Writers often have difficulty accommodating an audience; as they answer your questions and clarify their writing for you, they will learn how to adapt their texts for an audience.

## THE COUNSELOR

A student's life includes much more than the writing assignment at hand, and often other issues and concerns interfere with completing the assignment. Sometimes you may find yourself playing the role of counselor, listening to writers' concerns and dealing with such issues as attitude and motivation. You may encounter a transfer student who is disgruntled because she has lost credits in changing schools, a returning student who wonders if he can continue to juggle his job and school successfully, or a graduating senior who has lost interest in school and just can't seem to get motivated. In such cases, you offer support, sympathy, and suggestions as appropriate. You refer students to workshops or programs on campus: for example, conversation groups for learners of English as a second language, time-management or study-skills seminars, résumé workshops, or GRE reviews.

You may encounter a writer whose paper is deeply personal and reveals worrisome content that makes you feel uncomfortable or ill-prepared to address. If you think a student needs professional help, speak with your director or other administrator; he or she will know the appropriate campus resources and can refer the student.

# When Is a Tutor Not a Tutor?

Once your friends and neighbors—or even students you work with—realize that you are a writing tutor, they may seek your help with assignments outside the writing center. Except in special cases that only you can decide (helping a roommate or co-worker, for example), it is best to restrict your tutoring to the writing center. Otherwise, you may find yourself coerced into spending your study, sleep, or family time working on someone else's paper. If you have difficulty establishing boundaries with people requesting help outside of writing center hours, talk with your director or other administrator.

## Exercises for Exploring the Roles Tutors Play

### EXERCISE 3A    Exploring Tutors' Roles

The roles described in this chapter are not the only ones that tutors play. Sometimes, you may find yourself functioning as parent, therapist, actor, guru, or comedian. Exploring these potential roles can be interesting and informative.

Make a list of all the roles you can imagine tutors playing, then list the strengths and weaknesses of each: What is positive or negative about each role? How do these strengths and weaknesses affect tutoring? If you are working with other tutors, you might do this exercise in groups, with each group exploring the same or different roles.

### EXERCISE 3B    Observing Tutors' and Writers' Body Language

View a video of a tutoring session with the sound off. Alternately, watch ten minutes of a situation comedy, drama, or interview on television, again with no sound. Observe the body language and facial expressions of the tutor and writer or characters. What messages are communicated? How?

### EXERCISE 3C    Observing Tutoring Sessions

Observe several experienced tutors in sessions as they work with writers. (Be sure to get permission to sit in from both tutor and writer first.) Notice how tutors greet writers and establish rapport. Pay attention to the ways in which tutors learn what writers want help with and decide what to work on. How does the tutor engage the writer, phrase questions, and respond to the writer's concerns? What does body language convey about tutors and writers? How is a session ended?

If you are an online tutor, read chat sessions or advice from experienced tutors. How do they use questions in their advice? What is the tone of their advice? How do they explain difficult concepts? What kinds of examples do they use?

When each session ends, talk with the tutor. Ask specific questions about how and why the tutor conducted the session as he or she did. You may want to complete a form like the one on page 34 for each session you observe.

## Exercises for Practicing Tutoring Techniques

The following role-playing activities will help you to practice the tutoring techniques that are discussed in this chapter. If you are not using this book in conjunction with a class or training program, try to gather a group of tutors from your writing center who are willing to participate.

## EXERCISE 3D  Role-Playing the Tutoring Session

In pairs, role-play a "tutor" and "writer" starting a tutoring session. You can also role-play a synchronous chat by logging on to two separate computers. The tutor can simply play himself or herself and practice the following techniques:

- Greeting a writer and building rapport
- Getting information from the writer
- Assessing the needs of the writer
- Setting the agenda and determining a plan of action
- Setting boundaries for the session
- Using active listening
- Wrapping up the session

"Writers" should adopt one of the personas listed in the next section but without telling the tutor which one.

Follow-up discussion should focus on the reactions and behavior of both tutor and "writer." How did you feel during the session? What made you comfortable or uncomfortable? What seemed to be successful, frustrating, helpful, and not helpful? How was body language evident in the session? How might the tutor have handled things differently? Though not necessary, it can be useful to videotape sessions for later viewing and analysis.

### The "Writers"

1.  You don't like the writing assignment you've been given—a comparison and contrast of two similar persuasive arguments for the same issue: revising the movie-rating system. It doesn't make sense to you. Wouldn't it be better to look at two opposing opinions? Couldn't you pick your own topic? You also don't like your teacher. You think she's mean and withdrawn. If only she would just tell you what she wants, you could just do it. You're asking a tutor for help with your assignment, but what you really want is empathy and sympathy. Isn't this a terrible assignment? Isn't she a terrible teacher?

2.  You've got your paper drafted and are fairly comfortable with it. You know that it probably needs to be tweaked a bit here and there to improve it, but that's about all. The professor has said that he expects a strong introduction, and you know that yours could be a bit better. You also feel like your conclusion is too much of a rehash of what you just said. You're very open to suggestions and really expect that the tutor can give you some good advice.

3.  You are a brand-new freshman, you don't really know anyone very well yet, and so far college has been a far more scary experience than you'd thought it would be. You've been required to come to the writing center; otherwise, you would be in your dorm room, probably calling your parents or a close friend back home—again. You suspect that your

---

## TUTOR OBSERVATION SHEET

Your name:_____

Tutor's name: _____

Date:_____ Length of session:_____

Class student's paper is for, or other reason for coming to the center:

_____

_____

Description of the assignment:_____

Areas covered in the session:

What helped the student or worked in the session?

What was tried but didn't help the student or didn't work?

Comments and reflections on the session:

Final thoughts:

writing skills are pretty good because you did well in high school, but you wonder about how your writing compares with that of other freshmen. You hover near the door, unsure if you can muster the strength to enter the center. You barely speak above a whisper—if possible, not at all.

4. Fifteen years ago, you went to college for a couple of years, but you were unsure about what you wanted to do and finally quit. Now you're back in school and serious about getting a degree in education. But oh, that hiatus! You're very worried about your writing skills. Can you hold your own? What's the competition like? You're afraid you'll get a bad grade on this assignment. The paper is due in a week. You have brainstormed, outlined, and drafted. You suspect that there have been significant advances in approaches to writing over the past fifteen years, though you have no idea what those might be. You also have to pick up your children from school in an hour.

5. Swamped with several papers to write within the next two weeks, you have a ten-page history paper due today at noon. You got the research done for the history paper and finally sat down at 9:00 p.m. last night to write. At 5:00 a.m., you realized that you had good information, but you just weren't putting it together effectively. A couple of hours of sleep and now here you are, practically banging on the writing center's door and begging for help. In your sleep-deprived delirium, this paper has taken on extra importance. If you don't do well on it, you won't do well in the class. If you don't do well in the class, you won't do well in school. If you don't do well in school, you won't be able to get a job. It's 8:55 right now; if you can get some help by 9:30, you can get home by 10:00, revise and edit by 11:00, then a half hour for the bibliography... where IS everybody who works here?

6. Teachers (and tutors) represent authority to you. After all, they know so much more than you do. You've been brought up not to question authority. Even if you don't understand what a tutor says, you won't ask questions or seek clarification. If the tutor asks you something, you smile and try quietly to cover up your lack of understanding. You expect that the tutor will take your paper, read it, and use his or her expertise to edit it during the session.

7. You're an economics graduate student, and you've just started the first semester of the MS program. You feel confident in your field but have struggled with writing for as long as you can remember. You just can't seem to translate your ideas and thoughts into a coherent paper. You are nervous about an upcoming research proposal and bring your draft to the writing center. You don't care if the person reviewing your proposal understands the content; you just want to make sure that you've expressed yourself clearly.

8. You're actually a rather flaky person. If someone asks you about subject A, you find some obscure relation to subject B and discuss that. (For example, in your paper praising golfer Tiger Woods, you leap to discussing your love of sports, especially soccer. Mention of your experiences on the high-school team leads you into talk about an extracurricular activity, like the club sponsored by your favorite English teacher, which leads you to discuss what your favorite book was senior year.) You want help with this paper for your psychology class but just can't seem to focus on Jung's theories. You're likely to end up talking about anything but Jung in this session.

9. You are required to come to the writing center, and fulfilling this requirement is your main goal. You aren't much interested in the tutor's advice. The paper is due tomorrow, and you have the sketchiest of rough drafts, but you envision completing it easily in an hour or two this evening. You suspect that if you hand something in on time, you will receive a passing grade on it as well as in the class. At this moment, however, more than anything else, you want to be at home watching the basketball game on television. It's starting right about now. You have nothing against the tutor or the instructor, but you'll say anything to get the session over with.

10. You arrive at the writing center with a freshly printed copy of a paper for an English literature course. You are determined to get an A on this paper, so it must be letter-perfect. In taking advantage of this service for students, you assume that the tutor will scrutinize every sentence, every word, and every punctuation mark. You expect nothing less and won't be satisfied until your paper is flawless.

11. You've always had difficulty with being organized and meeting deadlines. Your first paper in a freshman writing course is due this afternoon. As you sit with the tutor, you struggle to remember where in your bag you put your two-page, handwritten rough draft, and a search of your backpack yields only page two. When you talk to the tutor about the paper, you have difficulty remembering your topic and the points that you argued. As things become more confusing, you look to the tutor to save you from the mess you've created.

12. Everyone in your entomology class is required to visit the writing center with the final draft of a paper on how climate influences insect populations. In addition to the assignment sheet, the teacher has provided a lengthy list of general requirements that pertain to writing (no contractions, no jargon or slang, no misspellings, no incomplete sentences, no prepositions before commas or at ends of sentences, and so on). You're not sure if your paper explains the influence of climate adequately. You also want to make certain that your paper follows all of the requirements on the list.

13. You believe that you're a good writer, but you want to make sure the paper on Gilbert Stuart portraits for your art history course is as good as it can be. You've made an appointment at the writing center and are willing to listen to any suggestions that the tutor may have. You've noticed a sign in the center asking that cell phones be turned off, but you've ignored it. Several minutes into the session, your phone rings. You answer, and it's a friend whom you've been anxious to reach. After a moment, you excuse yourself and seek a more private place (perhaps around a corner or in the hall) where you can talk.

14. You're researching a historical figure for a course on local history. You have several sources (all Web sites), but as you work on the paper, you realize that you're depending heavily on one. As you explain to the tutor, you've searched the campus library Web site and the Internet and didn't find anything more. Is this OK? If not, how should you go about finding more detailed sources so that you are not relying on just one for the entire paper?

15. You are a transfer student. In order to be exempt from the first-year writing requirement at the college you now attend, you must submit a portfolio of work completed in a similar course at another school in another state. You want to be sure that your papers are acceptable, so you've made an appointment at the writing center. You assume that a tutor will be familiar with the first-year writing requirement at the school and that he or she can tell you if anything needs to be changed.

16. You and two other students have met to work on a group paper that's due in three hours. When a question arises about the correct format for documenting one entry, you disagree with the others in the group. Since the writing center is nearby, the three of you decide to ask an "expert." All the tutors are busy, so you interrupt a tutor with your "quick question."

17. You're writing a personal narrative about a difficult situation that you've encountered. You chose to describe your problems with a learning disability (or health problem), but because it's a significant issue for you, you find it difficult to write about. You want a decent grade on this paper, but you've resorted to being aloof and sometimes sarcastic because your frustration and anger get in the way as you write. Why do you have to explain everything? Shouldn't people just understand? Also, how "personal" should a personal narrative be? How will you know what to include and what to leave out?

18. You're getting started on a twenty-page paper for a graduate seminar in sociology. As an immigrant yourself, you want to explore how immigrants negotiate the territory between their old and new cultures. Your thinking is still fuzzy, but you believe that fictional works describe

what happens well, while researchers tend to establish categories that leave gaps. What should you do? How should you proceed?

19. Your native language isn't English, but you've studied grammar and know the rules. Still, when you write, there are many mistakes. Your business teacher has failed your paper based on grammatical problems, but she says your content and organization are "quite good" and has allowed you to revise the paper. While you're grateful, you vaguely feel that she's discriminating against you because you are an international student. Still, you need a good grade on this paper because it's in your major.

20. You were assigned a group-written project in your sociology class. As usual with group projects, you felt that you did most of the work. What's more, the minor contributions from the rest of the group barely fit your style of writing. You want to see a tutor to help you better link the various sections and make them seem cohesive and written with one "voice."

### EXERCISE 3E   Role-Playing Tutor Strategies in the Prewriting Stage

This role-playing exercise will help you practice active listening, facilitating, and using silence and wait time. Some of you will play a tutor or writer; others will observe the tutor's actions and words. (Role players might want to take a few minutes to jot down notes before beginning.) Following are descriptions of the responsibilities for each role.

**Writer.**   Assume that you need to write a letter or a well-composed e-mail message on one of the topics listed on pages 39–40 and that you are seeking a tutor's help to explore your ideas and to begin arranging them effectively. You will need to anticipate readers' objections to the ideas that you express in the letter. Use your imagination to come up with convincing arguments and objections. (Note that you do not have to write the letter or e-mail, as you are in the preliminary stages of writing.)

**Tutor.**   The writer is seeking your help with writing a letter or an e-mail. Your task is to help the writer

- explore persuasive arguments,
- explore the audience's potential objections to those arguments and the writer's potential rebuttals to the objections, and
- begin planning an effective organization for the letter or e-mail.

At the same time, you must

- keep all of your ideas to yourself and make no contributions to the content or organization of the letter or e-mail, and
- pass no judgment on any of the ideas suggested by the writer. Ask questions that help the writer to focus and clarify ideas.

(Remember to practice active listening, facilitating, and using silence and wait time.)

**Observer(s).**  As the tutor works with the writer, look for examples of active listening, facilitative language, and silence or wait time. Make brief notes as you observe. (Your notes need not include a sentence's content, only enough to indicate that the tutor is being facilitative: "I can hear...," "What do you think?" and so on.) You may want to complete a form like the one on page 34 for the session that you observe.

Your group might want to try different topics, trading roles as you move to a new topic. Each participant would thus get a chance to be a tutor, a writer, and an observer. After each session, group members should talk about how it felt to play the different roles. Observers should also share their impressions. What strategies did tutors use, and how effective were they? How could tutoring sessions have been improved?

### Letter or e-mail topics

1. Spring semester is nearly over, and your parents have been looking forward to having you at home for the summer. But you wish to live and work away from home, perhaps at the beach or near your school. Select the place where you want to live for the summer, and write an e-mail to your parents explaining your reasons; try to convince them that your living away from home is a good idea.

2. A number of students who use the writing center have indicated the need for additional writing center hours. Write a letter to the director either supporting or opposing extended hours.

3. You really enjoy using the writing center at your school, but you juggle school, a job, and a family. You wish that the writing center would offer an online feature. Write an e-mail to the director asking that an online, interactive component be added to the writing center. Be particular about what features you'd like to see and describe their usefulness to students like you.

4. As the parent of a young child, you find that attending classes poses some difficulties. Write a letter to the president of your school requesting a day care facility for students' children. (If your school already has a day care facility, ask that its hours be extended or assume that it is in danger of being closed and ask that it remain open.)

5. Write a letter to the president of your school asking for a change from letter grades to pass-fail designations (or the opposite if your school already offers pass-fail courses).

6. You are determined to participate in an exercise program while you are home for the summer, but you know that you would be more apt to stick with it if you had company. Write an e-mail advocating a particu-

lar exercise program (such as swimming, weight training, or aerobics) to a friend who will also be home, asking him or her to join you.

7. You have an opportunity to attend a three-day conference for writing tutors, but one of your professors frowns on students' missing class. Write an e-mail to that professor explaining and justifying your request for an excused absence.

8. You and some friends have decided to travel for spring break. Write an e-mail to persuade your friends that swimming in Cancún would be better than skiing in Colorado. (Substitute other places and activities if you wish.)

9. Write a letter to the president of your school suggesting that a specific campus program be started or continued. (Some suggestions: an orientation course for new students, a writing center, a math center, a study-abroad program, a particular internship.)

10. Your parents do not think that it is a good idea for you to have a car on campus, but increasingly you wish to have one. Write an e-mail to your parents explaining your reasons.

11. Your younger brother or sister is considering buying a computer but is not sure whether to choose a laptop or desktop. Write an e-mail comparing the two options or explaining why one or the other is a better investment.

12. Your campus women's center is hosting a well-known speaker. As the student coordinator of the center, you need to arrange for facilities, food, and security. But first, you need funding! Write a letter to the dean of student life requesting money for this event. Make sure that you explain the rationale for the amount of funds being requested.

13. Your school is considering adopting an honor pledge to be written and signed on examinations, papers, or other academic assignments. The pledge reads: "I pledge on my honor that I have not given or received any unauthorized assistance on this assignment/examination." Write a letter to the editor of your school newspaper supporting or opposing the idea.

14. You recently bought a new DVD player but are unhappy with its overall quality. Write a letter of complaint to the manufacturer, and ask for a refund.

15. You strongly support a bill that will be coming before Congress soon. Write an e-mail to your senator expressing your support and explaining how the bill affects you.

4

# Helping Writers throughout the Writing Process

Like the writing process, tutoring is dynamic. The interaction between tutor and writer as questions, answers, and ideas flow back and forth largely determines the content and direction of any tutoring session. Face-to-face and synchronous online sessions develop as the writer and the tutor work together in real time; the dynamics of online asynchronous tutoring are somewhat different but no less fruitful. In asynchronous sessions, tutors can refer to previous sessions, online resources, and institutional resources while using a variety of technological strategies, like audio and video, to exchange ideas and help writers.

In Chapter 2, we reviewed the basic principles of the writing process—remember Tom, Keisha, Maria, Chu, and Miguel? Each writer was working his or her way through the writing process, sorting through ideas, getting them down on paper, and fine-tuning their presentation. This chapter provides some specific guidelines and strategies for working with writers at particular stages in the writing process.

What works with one writer, however, may not be as successful with another; therefore, you need to be ready with a variety of approaches and to be flexible about using them. As you become more proficient at tutoring, you will develop your own style and be able to add your own suggestions to those given here.

## Prewriting

### FINDING AND EXPLORING A TOPIC

Tutors can help writers discover what it is they want to say by using a variety of techniques. Brainstorming (listing), freewriting, and clustering (branching) are discussed here, but you may want to check writing handbooks and textbooks to learn about other techniques.

| | |
|---|---|
| SITUATION | Student is unsure about where or how to begin. |
| WHAT TO DO | Discuss.<br>Brainstorm.<br>Freewrite.<br>Collect, list, and select. |
| HOW TO RESPOND | Ask questions.<br>Reflect or mirror.<br>Offer suggestions.<br>Offer support. |

**Brainstorming (listing).**  Brainstorming involves focusing on a topic and tossing out, thinking through, and refining ideas to find ways to approach it. As writers list and play with ideas on a particular topic, ask questions to prod and encourage them to think more and reach further.

For example, tutor-in-training Andrea comes into the writing center for help in getting started on the "How I Write" assignment in Exercise 2E. Her tutor suggests that Andrea brainstorm a list of anything and everything that comes to mind when she thinks about writing. Andrea comes up with the following:

- wear comfortable clothes
- get my desk completely clear
- keep rereading the assignment description
- PROCRASTINATE
- write out some ideas on paper, put them on my computer, and move them around
- call my dad and read the paper to him
- write — rewrite — rewrite — rewrite
- make sure I have a strong (funny if possible) introduction
- put my hair in a ponytail
- try not to use a form of "to be" in the first sentence
- recall Ms. Coakley — my English teacher sophomore year

Following is Andrea's list reproduced again. The questions in parentheses are suggested questions that her tutor might ask to prompt her to think and generate more ideas.

- wear comfortable clothes  (Such as? Why?)
- get my desk completely clear  (Why?)
- keep rereading the assignment description  (When? To get started? As you write? Why? How does reading it over and over help you?)
- PROCRASTINATE  (Why did you put this word in caps? How do you procrastinate? What do you do? Why do you procrastinate?)

Shoe–New Business Macnelly. Distributed by King Features Syndicate.

- *write out some ideas on paper, put them on my computer, and move them around* (What do you mean by "move them around"? What do you do after that? Do you work only on the computer after that?)

- *call my dad and read the paper to him* (Why? How does that help?)

- *write – rewrite – rewrite – rewrite* (What do you mean by "write"? Why did you write "rewrite" three times?)

- *make sure I have a strong (funny if possible) introduction* (Why? How do you do that?)

- *put my hair in a ponytail* (Why? How does this relate to wearing "comfortable clothes"?)

- *try not to use a form of "to be" in the first sentence* (Why? How does this relate to having "a strong introduction"?)

- *recall Ms. Coakley – my English teacher sophomore year* (How did she affect your writing? What did you learn from her that affects your writing today?)

As writers' ideas evolve, paraphrase or mirror what you hear them saying in order to clarify, check, and sum up lines of thought. Pose questions that guide them toward considering the audience, such as "What does your audience know about...?" or "How can you make that clear to your audience?" You might also play devil's advocate and suggest an opposing viewpoint to writers. Responding to you will force them to examine their own ideas more thoroughly.

**Freewriting.** Ask writers to put pen to paper (or fingers to keyboard) and simply let ideas on the topic flow for ten minutes. Tell them to write words, phrases, sentences, or questions but to ignore punctuation and spelling. If they get stuck, tell them to rewrite the last few words over and over until the ideas begin to flow again.

Freewriting at the computer can be a quick and convenient way to get started. Allow the writer time to type in a list of ideas or thoughts on a topic. As you and the writer talk about the list and relationships among ideas emerge, these thoughts can be rearranged on the screen using cut and paste commands. Occasionally, people find it easier to freewrite on a screen

### Clustering Diagram

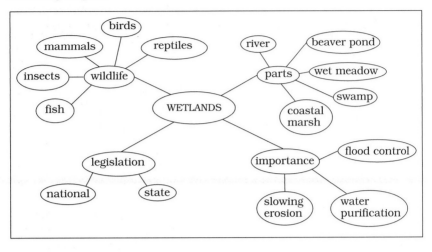

that remains blank (often the case with those who have writer's block); you can adjust the monitor's brightness (or turn it off) to accomplish this.

Take, for example, Zachary, who comes into the writing center with only a topic: tarot cards. His tutor sits him down at a computer, asks him to freewrite, and leaves him for five minutes. Zach comes up with the following paragraph.

> What do I know about tarot cards? You can tell your fortune with them. How accurate are they? I had this lady read mine at the Renaissance Festival last month. She was pretty accurate. I'm not sure how many there are. How do you learn to read them? Did anyone ever do any scientific investigation of them? Results? Where did they come from/start? Tarot cards. Tarot cards. The word "tarot" sounds unusual, maybe foreign. Do people all over the world use them? Sometimes in crossword puzzles — the word. What's on the cards? Pictures. Of what?

Zach and his tutor review together what Zach has written, looking for key words, phrases, or questions that seem promising. They focus on those and discuss or brainstorm. Zach's paragraph offers a wealth of details to explore further. The tutor might ask questions that will help Zach uncover more possibilities in key words and phrases like "accurate," "learn to read them," "foreign [word]," and "scientific investigation." Zach's reference to having tarot cards read at the Renaissance Festival might lead to questions about where others go to have tarot cards read.

**Clustering (branching or webbing).** Clustering not only helps writers explore their subject but also suggests how they might organize their ideas. With the writer, make a diagram with the central topic in the middle. Then, as you talk or chat with the writer about aspects of the topic, ask how each relates to the central topic and draw branches that show the relationships.

Effective with pen and paper, clustering also works especially well in online synchronous forums with drawing capabilities. In fact, using drawing tools, color, and highlight functions can help make these exercises more vivid for the writer.

The diagram on page 44 shows how one writer explored the topic of wetlands with a tutor. They began with the central topic—wetlands—in the middle. As they discussed aspects of the topic, the tutor asked questions about why and how each aspect related to the central topic. Eventually, the writer ended up with four issues related to wetlands: parts, wildlife, importance, and legislation—each of which had several sub-issues.

### Other suggestions for finding and exploring a topic

With most writers, asking probing questions and discussing the answers can be enough to help them explore and generate ideas about a topic. For those who find coming up with ideas more difficult, a different perspective or way of looking at a topic can be useful. Asking writers to engage in one of the following exercises will not generate a paper, but at the least, it will offer some avenues to investigate.

1. Imagine a scene that relates to the topic, and describe it. Try the same thing with a sound or smell.

2. Imagine yourself as someone else—your older brother, your mother, your boss. How would that person look at the topic? What would he or she say about it?

3. Write about the topic in an e-mail to someone with whom you feel comfortable.

4. If you could write this paper without constraints, what would you write about, and how would you go about it?

## PLANNING TO WRITE

Once writers have generated sufficient ideas to get started, you can help them to organize those ideas and to plan to write. A note of caution: Some writers want to begin organizing a paper when they have only a few sketchy ideas, but continuing down this trail usually leads to a weak paper. You can help writers avoid this pitfall by making sure that they have clearly identified their audience, their goal or purpose in relation to that audience, and what they hope to accomplish in the paper. If the writer has his or her assignment description, review the purpose and scope of the assignment, as well as the instructor's expectations. There are several ways you can help writers organize and plan.

1. Ask if they know the conventions of and formats for the kind of paper that they are working on. What does a cover letter accompanying a résumé typically include? What are the options for organizing a comparison and contrast paper or a definition paper? What should be

**Informal Outline**

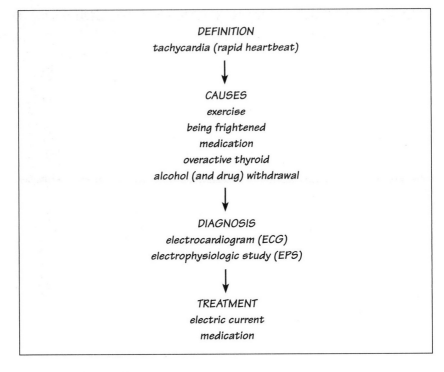

included in a lab report? If students are unsure, explain. If you also are unsure, check a handbook or guide to writing.

2. Help writers explore options by mapping out how the paper might be organized. Rather than make a formal outline, which can be too rigid and confining for many writers, suggest that the writer generate a more informal diagram, such as a list or flow chart similar to the one above. Writers can easily see the general shape of the paper but will feel more open to shuffling parts around if necessary.

3. Ask the writer to start drafting the thesis and topic sentences. It might be helpful to see the main ideas worked out in full sentences. These sentences can be a jumping-off point when the writer goes to compose on his or her own. Be sure to let the writer know that these sentences may be revised as she or he continues working on the paper.

## WORKING WITH A TEXT AT A COMPUTER

1. To make writers more aware of their writing patterns, use the highlight, underline, or bold commands. For example, ask writers who overuse forms of the verb *to be* to highlight all verbs in a portion of the text.

## Working with a Text at a Computer

You can then explain how to rephrase or combine sentences in order to achieve more vigor and variety.

2. As you discuss the concept of providing support for ideas, have writers highlight the main idea or topic sentence in each paragraph. They can then see if each remaining sentence in the paragraph supports that idea.

3. Using the Return or Enter key, writers can break a portion of their text down into sentences. This separation allows them to concentrate on smaller units and to see problems that sometimes get lost in standard text. In this way, you and the writer can look at matters of style (like sentence length and variety), coherence (like transitions from one sentence to another), and syntax (like fragments, comma splices, run-on sentences, and parallelism). The writer can also isolate whole paragraphs and then look specifically at the sentence order in each paragraph to consider rearranging them.

4. Likewise, the writer can cut and paste the main idea (a key phrase) from each paragraph. After moving these key phrases to the end of the text, the writer can create a kind of outline of the paper. From there, you and the writer can consider such matters as the thesis statement, organization, coherence, and evidence.

## Writing, Revising, and Editing

### MAKING GLOBAL REVISIONS

Global revisions refer to the paper's overall development and organization. When helping a writer make global revisions, consider if the paper addresses the topic in a meaningful way and if it has a logical flow.

### Development

Did the writer follow through on points raised in the thesis?

Did the writer offer enough supporting details and examples?

Did the writer explain relationships between ideas?

### Organization

Did the writer organize according to a particular scheme or format?

Did the writer organize according to the needs of a specific audience?

By first asking questions and talking with the writer about his or her paper's audience, topic, content, and structure, you get useful information and also give the writer the opportunity to indicate troublesome areas. As you then read through the paper together, you can compare what he or she has told you with what is actually on the page.

| | |
|---|---|
| **SITUATION** | Writer has a draft.<br>Writer has time to revise. |
| **WHAT TO DO** | Find out where the writer feels the draft needs improvement.<br>Point out where the draft needs improvement.<br>Explore possibilities. |
| **HOW TO RESPOND** | Question.<br>Reflect or mirror.<br>Offer suggestions and opinions. |

One of you should read the paper aloud. Asking writers to read aloud engages them more in the tutoring session; however, explain that you will interrupt whenever you have a question or comment. Occasionally, you may prefer to read, reacting and commenting as you go. In any case, do not simply let writers sit there and watch you read silently, for that will only increase any discomfort that they may be feeling.

As writers talk about their ideas or read aloud, ask questions or make comments in order to help them clarify their thinking and offer suggestions for improvement. Be an active listener, and reflect what you hear after the writer has spoken. For example, you might respond with a statement like "What I'm hearing you say is that your audience is composed of other computer science majors, and you're trying to convince them that...." At this stage, focus on the larger issues of content and organization. Not only are they more important than matters of style or mechanics but you might also end up spending much of the tutoring session on a section that is ultimately deleted.

If you are tutoring online, you may not be able to communicate immediately with the writer; however, that should not prevent you from asking questions. Let the writer know your reaction as a reader. Consider modeling your comment like "I think you're trying to refer back to the thesis here, but I'm not sure. Can you make that connection more explicit?" The first statement will alert the reader to the global problem; the question will provide a starting place as the writer attempts to address the problem.

As you go through the paper together, you may be able to identify places where the argument is unsubstantiated, where the writer may need to conduct further research in order to find and incorporate more compelling sources. If you see an idea that is lacking support, consider logging on to the library's home page and helping the writer conduct a database search. (For more about online research, see Chapter 6.)

### Other suggestions for global revision

1. Read the paper as a naive reader, and indicate those places where it needs more details or more specific details. For example, if you read a sentence like "Watching the university's production of *Hamlet* was an exciting experience," ask what the writer means by "exciting." What exactly was it about this production that made seeing it exciting? If you read something such as "My grandfather was a kind and generous person," ask for some specific examples or anecdotes that demonstrate his kindness and generosity.

2. Stop at the end of a paragraph or section of the paper to summarize what you have just read and to explain what you anticipate will follow. If what you say does not match the writer's intended message, he or she can see where misinformation, extraneous details, or other cues misdirect the reader.

3. Don't overwhelm the writer with too many suggestions for improvement at one time. First, see if you can identify the major recurring issues that impede the readability of the paper. Then, try to find one or

two sections or sentences that represent these issues, and spend some time working with the writer on these smaller pieces of the paper. If the writer seems frustrated, it may be better to select problems that are fairly easy to deal with in order to give him or her a more successful tutoring session. You can indicate that other areas need work and suggest that the writer make another appointment to attend to them.

### Revising at the Computer

The computer makes it easy to revise without erasing, scribbling out, or trying to fit new thoughts or ideas in cramped spaces above and below the existing text.

1. Using the Return or Enter key, the writer can double or even triple space to gain room to insert comments, options, or definitions above or below the appropriate place in the text. Or, the writer can insert a revised version of part of the text above or below the original to compare and choose. He or she can also leave large blank spaces in appropriate spots for further development of the text.

2. Most word processing programs have a reviewing or editing function that allows the writer to track changes throughout the text. The writer can also insert comments to help remember the major points that you discuss in the tutoring session. These comments will appear in the margins and are thus easily distinguishable from the rest of the text.

### Saving Multiple Drafts

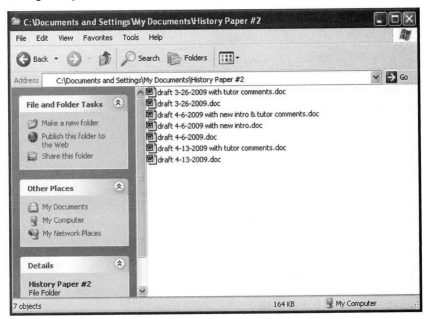

### Saving Multiple Drafts

Writers go through several drafts as they develop their writing, but they do not always keep each of those drafts. Encourage writers to save multiple, dated versions of their work instead of overwriting a single draft again and again. These earlier drafts provide a tangible record of how far a writer has come since the beginning of the writing process and may be useful if a professor wants a look at past drafts to ensure that the paper is entirely the writer's own work.

Revisiting earlier drafts may also inspire new ways of thinking as a writer struggles with a current draft. Is there a forgotten insight that might be expanded? Could an idea or point that was dropped initially be reintegrated into the current draft? Asking such questions may lead the writer to consider the current draft or some ideas for it in new ways.

## MAKING SENTENCE-LEVEL REVISIONS

Sentence-level revisions involve strengthening and varying sentences as well as refining style. Inappropriate or imprecise language, wordiness, and choppiness are common problems in student papers. To help writers recognize these problems and learn to correct them, concentrate on a small section—a paragraph or several sentences. Later, writers can apply what they have learned to the rest of the paper. This approach also reminds writers that they are ultimately responsible for revising their papers.

Online tutors should be careful not just to correct mistakes but also to explain how writers can identify and correct future sentence-level errors. Although the reviewing function in word processing programs can be helpful, avoid editing the paper. Rather, copy and paste a problematic sentence or two into your comments, identify the mistake(s), and provide feedback.

### Other suggestions for sentence-level revision

1. To improve the voice of the paper, ask the writer, "Do you talk like this?" Discuss the use of language in the paper, and then help the

| SITUATION | Writer has a satisfactory draft. |
|---|---|
| | Writer has time and motivation to revise. |
| WHAT TO DO | Read carefully, preferably aloud. |
| | Consider each paragraph, sentence, and word. |
| HOW TO RESPOND | Help in reading. |
| | Point out kinds of problems. |
| | Question. |
| | Mirror and reflect. |
| | Offer opinions and suggestions. |
| | Demonstrate techniques for improvement. |

writer rework a small section and eliminate, for example, stuffiness or stilted words and phrases. To make tone more appropriate in a formal paper, explain the conventions of formal writing. For example, explain that using contractions is inappropriate in a formal paper, as is the use of *etc.*

2. To eliminate wordiness, go through several sentences word by word with the writer to determine if each word is really necessary. You might also read wordy sentences back to the writer and then read the sentences again, leaving out what you think are excess words. Ask the writer to consider whether the words that you have omitted are necessary.

3. To improve choppy writing, have the writer read the paper aloud. (Often, it is easier for the writer to detect choppiness when reading aloud than when reading silently.) You might want to have the writer revise some problem sentences in the tutoring session.

4. If the writer tends to use several prepositional phrases in a row, read a few sentences aloud. As you read, accent the choppy effect that such phrases produce, and then show the writer how to eliminate at least some of the phrases. For example, changing "Running in the morning on the track on the campus keeps one fit" to "A morning run on the campus track keeps one fit" makes the sentence less choppy and less wordy yet retains the meaning.

5. Ask the writer to check his or her work for overuse of *to be* verb forms (such as *am, is, are, were*). He or she can improve emphasis by replacing these forms with more vigorous verbs and eliminating passive-voice constructions. If you notice that the writer overuses *to be* forms and the passive voice, ask him or her to circle all the verbs in a passage and then look at them and tell you what he or she notices.

6. For any of these sentence-level issues, take one of the writer's sentences, one of your own creation, or one from an exercise and demonstrate how making appropriate changes renders it more effective. Called *modeling*, this technique allows you to create several alternatives and to explain your reasoning for the changes.

## EDITING FOR GRAMMAR, PUNCTUATION, AND MECHANICS

Tutors often worry that they must be thoroughly familiar with grammar rules, but that is not true. Good readers usually recognize a problem, though they may not always be able to explain it technically. If you are unsure about a rule or term, check a guide to grammar, punctuation, and mechanics. Another handy and excellent reference that should not be overlooked is another tutor.

When you encounter problems with grammar, punctuation, or mechanics, paint a larger picture for writers. Explain that such errors distract readers

| SITUATION | Writer has a satisfactory draft. |
| | Writer has time and motivation to revise. |
| WHAT TO DO | Read carefully, preferably aloud. |
| | Consider each paragraph, sentence, and word. |
| HOW TO RESPOND | Help in reading. |
| | Point out kinds of problems. |
| | Question. |
| | Mirror and reflect. |
| | Offer opinions and suggestions. |
| | Demonstrate techniques for improvement. |

from the paper's content. If readers pause to notice misplaced commas or misspellings, they lose the thread of the paper for a moment and must reorient themselves to continue reading. In the process, the paper's content may become less compelling.

As you discuss grammatical points, be flexible with your vocabulary. What one writer knows as a "fused" sentence another calls a "run-on." In addition, writers may be unfamiliar with terms like *comma splice* or *independent clause*. When you use technical terms, ask the student if she or he needs a definition of the term or further clarification. If you are tutoring online and use a technical term, consider embedding a link with the definition and explanation of the term.

In *Teaching One-to-One: The Writing Conference*, Muriel Harris suggests turning the process of understanding over to writers by offering enough explanation to start them off and then inviting them to "find and revise all instances of whatever problem was discussed, asking questions as they proceed; to reformulate the principle for themselves in terms that they are comfortable with; to write their own sentences demonstrating the rule; to cite uses of the rule in their own papers if that seems helpful; or to explain how the rule works in their sentence."[1] If serious problems with grammar, punctuation, and mechanics permeate a student's paper, concentrate on a small section—a paragraph or several sentences—to help the writer recognize and learn to correct these errors. Later, the writer can go through the rest of the paper and apply what he or she has learned.

### Other suggestions for editing grammar, punctuation, and mechanics

1. Have writers read their papers aloud. In doing so, they often make corrections as they go, for the ear frequently judges more accurately than the eye. In addition, their changes afford you the opportunity to encourage them by pointing out that they really do know how to recognize and correct some of their errors.

---

[1]Muriel Harris. *Teaching One-to-One: The Writing Conference*. Urbana: NCTE, 1986, 120.

2. Point to an error and ask a general question, such as "Do you see a problem here?" You might underline several sentences that reflect the same problem and ask the writer to read them aloud. If the writer cannot see the problem, focus on a single sentence. If he or she still remains uncertain, explain the error and see if he or she can identify it elsewhere.

3. Ask writers to indicate which sentences they feel uncomfortable with and then ask why.

## Using a Handbook

A handbook serves as a concise and ready reference or manual on a particular subject. The late Diana Hacker described *The Bedford Handbook* as "small enough to hold in your hand... [and able to] answer most of the questions you are likely to ask as you plan, draft, and revise a piece of writing."[2] Whether seeking general help on new ways to think about narrowing a topic or more specific advice on a grammatical point or documentation, even the best writers frequently consult a handbook; no one knows all the answers by heart. As you work with writers, do not hesitate to consult a handbook and suggest that they bring their own handbooks to future tutoring sessions. Together, you can tag sections that writers may want to reference again as they continue to revise. Not only can you help them answer their questions accurately, but you will also be modeling the behavior of good writers.

## Coping with the Long Paper

Sometimes, writers find the task of writing a longer paper to be somewhat daunting. When they cannot complete the paper in one or two sittings, they can become overwhelmed by the task. As a tutor, you can offer suggestions not only for planning, organizing, and writing but also for coping with the process in general. Chapter 8 offers some additional guidelines for tutoring longer papers.

### Some suggestions for coping with the long paper

1. Briefly discuss the writer's writing process with him or her. When is the writer's optimum time for accomplishing a writing task? Early morning, when he or she is fresh? Late at night, so he or she can continue working if inspiration strikes? Help the writer to determine the best time to work and to plan accordingly.

---

[2]Diana Hacker. *The Bedford Handbook*, 7th ed. Boston: Bedford/St. Martin's, 2006, xxv.

2. Help the writer break the larger task of "writing the paper" into a series of smaller, more easily achievable tasks. The list might begin as follows: Determine a broad or tentative topic, research to see what material is available, reassess the topic and narrow it, draft an introduction, roughly outline the rest of the paper, and so on. Then, discuss planning each working session—research or writing—as another list of tasks, ones that can be accomplished within that time. The idea is to plan for achieving a sense of accomplishment and progress. In two hours, for example, it is doubtful that the writer will finish the paper, but he or she can think through and draft an introduction, then sketch out roughly what the rest of the paper might look like. Accomplishing these smaller goals allows the writer to feel some measure of success and progress.

3. Offer specific suggestions to make each writing session successful. For example, many of us procrastinate by doing tasks that enable us to avoid writing. Suggest that writers set a time limit for working—a kind of contract with themselves—and stick to it: "I will work from 7:00 to 10:00 p.m." The promise of a reward at the end—updating a Facebook page, watching a television show, or eating a bowl of ice cream—increases the incentive to keep working.

4. Suggest that when writers finish working for the day, they take a few moments to plan the subsequent session. Deciding where to begin next gives the following session direction from the outset and enables writers to start work immediately.

5. Remind writers that writing is a process. They should pay attention initially to larger issues of content and organization, leaving concerns about sentence length and variety, spelling, punctuation, and the like for later.

## Exercises for Using Writing References

### EXERCISE 4A    Exploring Prewriting Strategies

There are many strategies to use in prewriting. Check a handbook or writing textbook to learn about other techniques. Then, choose one and explain it to other tutors, showing how they might use it in tutoring. If time allows, demonstrate the technique.

### EXERCISE 4B    Developing a Handout

Individually or in small groups, develop a handout or online resource that you and other tutors might use with writers. The handout may offer help with a stage of the writing process, discussing, for example, prewriting techniques, or it may explain and offer an exercise for a grammatical point. As you work, keep your audience firmly in mind. Make sure that your explanations are clear and complete and that your vocabulary is appropriate for the writers with whom you work. Do not make the mistake of one tutor, a sports buff, who in an effort to generate interest developed an exercise using sports jargon; writers unfamiliar with some terms found the exercise confusing.

### EXERCISE 4C    Working with Handbooks and Other References

When you are tutoring, questions will come up that you cannot answer on your own. You may be uncertain about the parts of a proposal, a rule for using semicolons, or documentation according to the American Psychological Association (APA) format. In these cases, you may have to check references as you help writers. Such resources vary from writing center to writing center, but most centers have a collection of writing guides and handbooks, a list of helpful online resources, and a file of explanations and exercises.

To familiarize yourself with the resources available at your writing center, explore them and note at least two places—one text-based and one online—where you could find the following information:

1. accepted formats for business letters
2. an explanation and exercise on subject-verb agreement
3. discussion of thesis statement, with examples
4. strategies for tightening wordy sentences
5. guidelines for evaluating a Web site
6. rules for when to spell out numbers or use figures
7. exercises for correcting comma splices
8. advice on writing and formatting résumés
9. a discussion of subordination for emphasis
10. an explanation of cause and effect as a pattern of development
11. guidelines for putting together a PowerPoint presentation

12. the format for documenting a selection in an anthology using the Modern Language Association (MLA) style

13. the rules for use of *who* and *whom*

14. ways to avoid using sexist language

15. a list of common spelling errors

16. an explanation of passive and active voice

17. the conventions for referring to authors in the text of a literary paper

18. a list of logical fallacies with explanations and examples

19. guidelines for creating an entry in an annotated bibliography

20. information on what to consider with scannable résumés

21. explanations and examples of paraphrasing effectively

22. the correct spelling for the past tense of *cancel* and *travel*

23. information on e-mail etiquette ("netiquette")

24. rules for subject-verb agreement with collective nouns like *committee, audience,* and *couple*

25. rules for using abbreviations with proper names

# 5

# The Writers You Tutor

The writers you tutor will have varied learning styles, attitudes, backgrounds, and competencies that affect their thinking and behavior. Some writers — those with writing anxiety, basic writing skills, or learning disabilities or those for whom English is a second language, or adult learners — may present special challenges for tutors. Knowing specific approaches or strategies for assisting these writers makes sessions with them more beneficial and productive. In addition, we think you will find that many of the strategies and approaches can be useful in tutoring all writers.

One suggestion bears special mention because it applies to any writer who seeks help from a writing tutor: Regard and discuss the paper that the writer presents as a rough draft. The term *rough draft* can apply to a spectrum of writing in the drafting and revising process, including notes, loosely organized paragraphs, or even the writer's fourth revision. Regardless of how messy or clean the draft is, think and talk about it as a work in progress, one that is full of promise and potential. This stance allows you to discuss aspects of the paper in terms of what might be more effective instead of what is inadequate or wrong.

Writers do not always think of their papers as drafts, and while they may request suggestions for improvement, they may not be immediately receptive to your advice. Though they may not articulate or even recognize it, their writing is quite personal and sharing it can make them feel vulnerable. Their drafts represent authorial decisions they have made, which can lead to their taking criticism more personally than it is intended. This sensitivity can be particularly acute for first or early drafts, the likes of which may present many areas for improvement. As a tutor, try to frame the negative aspects of a paper as good first steps toward improvement and offer lots of encouragement. For example, a paper may lack organization but present several good ideas. Start with those good ideas and help the writer reorganize. Or, the writer may make a claim that is unsubstantiated. Praise him or her for the interesting claim, but then ask the writer to provide more support for that claim. Furthermore, point to successful aspects of the paper in order to encourage and support the writer. Perhaps you can point to a

## Calvin and Hobbes　　　　　　by Bill Watterson

specific focus, places where the audience is particularly well considered or an enticing introduction. Explain that the draft accomplishes much that is good and promising, and then enumerate those aspects.

How much nicer to treat the paper as a draft and discuss its potential than to regard it as a final copy and offer only negative comments! Praise and affirmation always feel good; we like to hear that we've attempted something and done it well, even as we recognize that we could do it better. Feeling successful in some areas allows writers to more easily continue working to improve in other areas, and tutors are in a perfect position to facilitate and encourage writers, especially those who struggle. It is also worthwhile to remind ourselves that learning styles and cultural background, as well as events in daily life, affect the ways each of us handles a writing assignment. You might never know about some of these influences (a writer's concerns about family or financial problems, for example), but it is important to be aware that such concerns may exist. As you work with individuals, your words and actions should convey sensitivity and understanding; each writer deserves to be treated fairly and with respect.

## Learning Styles

In previous chapters, you looked at the ways in which you and other tutors complete writing tasks. You doubtlessly discovered that each person has a different approach, and the same is true of the ways we learn. We tend to assume that others learn the way we do and are sometimes mystified when explanations or approaches that make perfect sense to us do not click with them. But not everyone absorbs and retains information in the same way, and different writers respond to different tutoring strategies.

At the most basic level, people learn by seeing (visual), by hearing (auditory), and by doing (kinesthetic, which is the Greek word for *movement*). Usually, writers are aware of their personal learning styles and can communicate to you how they best learn. Remember that people retain more of what they learn when they are actively involved and engaged in the process. With some writers, it may be appropriate to ask if they learn best by seeing, hearing, or doing. If you have trouble getting through to a student with one technique—say, simply talking over a draft—you might want to try another approach, perhaps jotting down notes, creating an informal outline, or drawing diagrams. As you become more familiar with the writers who visit your writing center and have a chance to try different approaches, you will gain a better sense of what they respond to best.

## SOME HELPFUL STRATEGIES

### Visual Strategies

1. Rather than simply talking, work from written material, pointing to, circling, highlighting, or otherwise indicating information as you discuss it.

2. Make writing things down a part of the tutoring session by taking notes, jotting down examples, or drawing diagrams. When writers leave, they will have something to take along—visual reminders of what you have discussed with them.

3. Use color when possible—different colored pens or, if working on the computer, highlighting or different colored fonts when inserting new text.

4. Separate a passage into individual sentences on the computer and use some of the other suggestions in "Working with a Text at a Computer" on page 47 in Chapter 4.

### Auditory Strategies

1. Read instructions, notes, or other material aloud, or have writers read aloud.

2. Repeat or rephrase directions and explanations, especially ones that may be more complicated.

3. Verbally reinforce points made in notes, diagrams, or other visual aids.

4. Throughout the session, ask the writer to paraphrase what you have discussed; at the end of the session, ask the writer to summarize what was accomplished and outline his or her plan for the paper.

5. If working online asynchronously, consider using software to embed an audio file to supplement your written advice.

### Kinesthetic Strategies

1. As you read through papers or discuss ideas, ask students to do the writing, underlining, highlighting, or diagramming.

2. Have students point to material as you talk about it.

3. Write sentences or sections of a paper on self-stick removable notes, separate pieces of paper, or file cards or even cut the paper apart. Ask

students to rearrange the passages in order to find the most effective organization.

4. Have self-stick removable notes on hand, and use them to identify parts of the paper, like the thesis, topic sentences, and evidence. Have the student write the concept on the self-stick note and then match it to the appropriate part of the paper.

## Student Concerns

If you have ever tried to write a paper after a fight with your parents or a close friend, when you are frantic about another course, or when coping with a difficult roommate, then you know that writing can be influenced by factors in your life other than school.

The following chart shows some common concerns of college students. As you look through it, think about the students who come to the writing center. Consider that, at various times, students may have additional anxieties. For example, first-year or transfer students are adapting to a new school; many sophomores are choosing a major; seniors are facing job searches and increased independence; and returning students are coping with school, family, and job responsibilities. Though you cannot—and would not want to—be privy to all of their concerns, it is good to remind yourself of the various personal issues that can affect students' writing.

**ACADEMIC CONCERNS**

| | | |
|---|---|---|
| Competition | Study skills | Classes (size, difficulty) |
| Grades | Test anxiety | School size, bureaucracy |
| Family's or personal expectations | | |

**SOCIAL CONCERNS**

| | |
|---|---|
| Roommates | Separation from family and friends |
| Friendships | Dating and relationships |
| Sexuality | Peer pressure |

**LIFESTYLE CONCERNS**

| | | |
|---|---|---|
| Independence | Living arrangements | Privacy |
| Job responsibilities | Finances | Family issues |
| Health concerns | | |

## The Writer with Writing Anxiety

Kathy panics the moment she hears the words "write a paper." Rather than take notes as the teacher gives instructions, she tunes out the details and thinks only about the monumental task of producing a paper. As she leaves class, Kathy frantically asks her classmates, "What are we supposed to do?

How long is it? When is it due?" Kathy has writing anxiety, which can take many forms. One writer frets because he cannot produce a polished piece of writing in one sitting. Another writer dislikes writing so much that she puts off getting down to work and finds herself approaching the deadline with little behind her but worry and procrastination. Still another writes and writes and writes, disheartened that he cannot get what he has to say "right."

Though the specific suggestions that you offer each of these writers may vary, it is always helpful to present yourself as a sympathetic ally. When Javon first came to the writing center, he described himself as "desperate." "Why can't I just sit down and write?" he asked. "Isn't that what everyone else does?" As he discussed his concerns with a tutor, she shared her own frustrations about writing, and Javon began to see that he was not alone. They worked together on his next few papers, and with his tutor's help, Javon figured out ways of addressing his writing anxiety so that he could become more productive and confident. Eventually, Javon decided that helping others with their writing would be rewarding—and would also help him develop even stronger skills—and he became a writing tutor himself. He was an especially good tutor because he understood the insecurities many writers face.

Likewise, you might tell students about some of your writing frustrations. Acknowledge that writing is indeed hard work, not only for them but for everyone. Just telling students that experienced writers often find it difficult to sit down and apply themselves can be surprisingly reassuring. Sharing details about the messiness of your own early drafts—the rambling introduction that suffices early on, the misspellings and poor grammar that you'll fix later—grants students permission to show and discuss their own tentative drafts without apology. But you should also tell them that the satisfaction of producing a well-written paper is enormously rewarding.

### Some strategies for working with a writer who has writing anxiety

1. Briefly explain the writing process. Point out that beginning as soon as possible and allowing plenty of time actually makes the task easier. Getting words on paper helps writers figure out what they want to say. Starting early also allows time for the unconscious mind to play with the ideas that have consciously been gathered.

2. Help writers break the assignment into a sequence of specific, manageable tasks. Then, help them set up a reasonable schedule with deadlines for completing the various parts. This planning will also enable writers to make use of the writing center during the writing process and can prevent small problems from becoming big ones.

3. Point out that breaking down the process of writing a paper into specific, manageable tasks can help writers feel degrees of success along the way. Rather than planning to sit down for an evening to "write the paper," a writer might set out to draft an introduction and work out a tentative organization for the rest of the paper or plan to revise a

particular section of the paper. Approaching tasks in this way enables writers to leave their desks with a sense of having accomplished what they set out to do, rather than with disappointment or frustration that the paper is not yet finished after several hours of work.

4. Suggest that writers set firm writing appointments with themselves and build in rewards. They can promise to work for a set period without interruptions and then get a reward at the end—a bike ride, a new DVD, a bowl of ice cream, or some other treat. Such rewards may sound silly, but the strategy often works.

5. Remind writers that a rough draft is exactly that: rough. Especially in the early stages, writing needs to be free flowing rather than perfect. Writers should be concerned with putting ideas on paper and not get bogged down with finding the "right" word or making each sentence perfect before beginning the next one.

## The Writer with Basic Writing Skills

In *Errors and Expectations*, Mina Shaughnessy illuminates the difficulties that writers with basic writing skills have producing effective academic writing. In this landmark book, Shaughnessy describes basic writers' problems with handwriting, punctuation, syntax, grammar, and spelling and then discusses the difficulties caused by their lack of familiarity with the concepts and forms of academic writing. Throughout this book and in her other publications about basic writing, Shaughnessy addresses the issue of the teacher's attitude. Repeatedly, she underscores the importance of respecting writers' intelligence, making the point that basic writers are not stupid but rather are uninformed or misinformed. Further, she points out that these writers do not necessarily apply grammatical rules incorrectly but instead use a different set of rules, acquired from speaking nonstandard English. Likewise, their writing reflects a lack of familiarity with the conventions for showing relationships among parts of a piece of writing rather than ignorance of the relationships themselves. As Shaughnessy explains,

> For the BW [basic-writing] student, academic writing is a trap, not a way of saying something to someone. The spoken language, looping back and forth between speakers, offering chances for groping and backing up and even hiding, leaving room for the language of hands and faces, of pitch and pauses, is generous and inviting. Next to this rich orchestration, writing is but a line that moves haltingly across the page, exposing as it goes all that the writer doesn't know, then passing into the hands of a stranger who reads it with a lawyer's eyes, searching for flaws.[1]

---

[1]Mina Shaughnessy. *Errors and Expectations*. New York: Oxford University Press, 1979, 7.

If you will be tutoring basic writers frequently, probably the best way to pre-pare is to read *Errors and Expectations*. In addition, you might look at other books and articles on basic writing.

## Some general suggestions for working with basic writers

1. Take care to be supportive, respectful, patient, and encouraging. Writers with basic writing skills often feel especially frustrated and even defeated by the task of writing. Be sure to acknowledge (and thus reinforce) what they do well, whether it's a larger issue like organization or a smaller issue like an especially appropriate phrase or word.

2. Talk with writers about their perceptions of writing and of the writing process. Help them understand that the writing process moves from the messy, tentative beginnings of formulating and ordering ideas to getting those ideas on paper and making meaning of them, first for the writer and then for the reader. By discussing the larger process, you reassure writers that they do not have to produce perfectly formed ideas and writing from the start. When you explain the editing stage, emphasize that this stage ensures that errors will not distract readers.

3. Help writers develop and convey meaning by explaining what you think they said in a sentence or passage. For example, after reading a concluding paragraph, you might say, "Your last paragraph says that you've shown four ways students can reduce stress, but I only remember three: [list them]. Did I miss one? Can you show me where it is?" By responding to writers in this way, you can help them see where the meaning of their writing does not match their intentions.

4. Look at the grammar and punctuation not in isolation but as a part of communicating ideas effectively. If a writer struggles to combine two sentences, use that example to talk about the appropriate punctua-tion rather than simply handing the writer an exercise on commas or semicolons.

5. Have writers read their papers aloud or into a digital tape recorder. Listening to themselves can help writers identify weaknesses in devel-opment, coherence, and sentence structure. This activity also reinforces and encourages writers' ability to recognize their own weaknesses — and their strengths.

6. Do not overwhelm writers with too much information or too many suggestions at once. It is better to cover one or two areas well so that writers can master them and feel successful. You can acknowledge other problems, but address them in later sessions.

7. If a writer has several problems, work with him or her to develop a strategy for coping with them. Make a plan for the next paper(s) and how to deal with grammatical and mechanical issues. Suggest

that the writer see a tutor early and regularly throughout the writing process.

You might begin with a session to clarify the assignment (purpose, scope, audience) and then schedule other sessions to work through prewriting, drafting parts of the paper, and revising—all according to the writer's needs. Likewise, list the other issues to attend to, prioritize them, make a plan of attack, and schedule future sessions. Be realistic, and do not overwhelm the writer. You might arrange to split each session between working on the paper and working on these other issues.

## The Second Language Writer

Becoming proficient in a second language is a slow process, and second language learners or writers, often referred to as English as a second language (ESL) writers, can sometimes pose a challenge for tutors. Their difficulties with composition involve not only language but also unfamiliar customs and ways of thinking that may be reflected in their writing or in their approaches to the writing process. Culture determines acceptable ways of presenting information, and in a tutoring session, acknowledging cultural differences often means explaining appropriate rhetorical patterns for standard academic English.

In some cultures, for example, the welfare of the group is more important than that of the individual, and the notion of individuals owning ideas may seem strange. Western cultures, however, embrace the individual and insist on careful attribution and documentation in written texts. Consequently, you may need to be sensitive to how you address academic integrity and frame your explanation within the unique rhetorical context of the Western university. Likewise, Americans tend to value a direct approach, but some cultures believe that meaning should be implied rather than spelled out directly. Other cultures approach a problem by giving a detailed history first, information that other writers might find unnecessary. One culture may lean toward exaggeration and emotionalism; another may do quite the opposite, focusing on restraint and understatement. These cultural differences often influence the rhetorical choices second language writers make in terms of content and strategies when they are writing in English. In addition, students from different cultures not only may have difficulty conceptualizing how to write for a Western audience—with emphases on thesis and argument as well as on conciseness and clarity—but also may be unsure about how to function in a Western university. Such difficulties may be reflected in their writing. While you want to be aware of cultural differences, you should not assume that every writer you meet from a particular culture embodies what you know about that culture. What is important is that, when you encounter these differences, you respect them for what they represent: unique ways of looking at the world.

## Korean Grammar

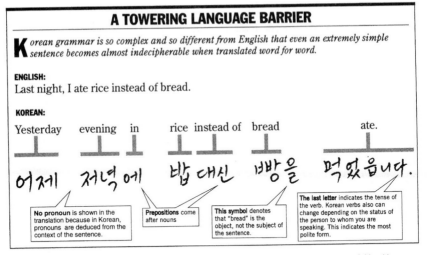

Furthermore, the grammatical issues that second language learners deal with are not homogeneous; rather, they may depend on an individual's native language and on previous instruction and experience in English. A writer whose native language does not include articles, for instance, may well have difficulty knowing when to use *a, an,* or *the.* Many problems that second language writers encounter occur because their first language follows different rules: For example, prepositions may not function as they do in English, the same rules of subject-verb agreement may not apply, or adjectives may follow rather than precede nouns. Additionally, some second language writers work diligently to master rules for English usage and can cite and apply grammar rules correctly in an exercise but have difficulty applying them as they write an essay. To get an idea of what some second language writers face as they attempt to acquire a second language, look at the example of Korean grammar in the figure above.

When you work with second language writers, respond first to the content and organization of their papers, as you would with any writer. Fixing sentences that may later be discarded wastes time. Read the description of the assignment and see if the paper adequately addresses the audience and fulfills the purpose. Listen to what writers are trying to say on paper and help them make sense of it.

Encourage writers to talk through what they want to say in each paragraph—in other words, to describe briefly each paragraph's focus and content. This nonevaluative approach is especially helpful with people who are unaccustomed to questioning authority (and to them, you are the authority in the tutoring situation). As you work with writers and their papers, ask questions that will help you understand what they are trying to communicate. Paraphrase what they say to see if you understand it correctly.

Be aware, however, that some writers may regard you as an expert and expect you to provide answers and simply fix the problems in their papers, putting you at cross purposes. As you ask the open-ended questions that aim to make writers responsible for their papers, they may sit, waiting to record answers. As Muriel Harris notes,

> [T]here may be a strained silence in a tutorial when a tutor asks and then waits patiently for answers to standard tutors' questions intended to give the students an active role, such as "How would you fix this paragraph?" or "What do you see as the problem here?" The tutor may interpret this silence as an indication that the student doesn't have an answer, but it may more likely be that the student is also sitting patiently, waiting for the tutor to fulfill his or her function of providing such answers. Some discussion is then necessary to help the student see that he or she really is being given an opportunity to learn by offering an answer.[2]

As you work with second language writers, remember that no one can absorb a great deal of information at one time. In fact, too much help can be overwhelming and can make writers feel even less secure. It is wiser to concentrate on one or two problems at a time so that writers can understand them and feel some degree of success. You can point out other problems, but leave them for subsequent tutoring sessions.

English can sometimes be illogical, and learning it can be difficult. As you work with writers, strike an appropriate balance between sympathy and encouragement. Sometimes, second language writers are serious students who do very well in some classes and are unaccustomed to encountering difficulties with a course; therefore, they find their problems with writing in English especially frustrating. Even as you show understanding of their problems, take special care to reinforce what they do know, and encourage them to learn and apply rules.

### Some suggestions for working with second language writers

The most important qualities you can bring to tutoring sessions with second language writers are patience and respect, and you can communicate those qualities through your words and actions. Recognize the difficulty of what they are trying to accomplish and how hard they work at it. But don't stop there; learn from them and enjoy doing so. As you work with second language writers, consider the following suggestions:

1. Beginning a tutoring session with a second language writer can have its own unique problems. Be aware that the writer may be especially apprehensive not only about showing you his or her writing but also

---

[2]Muriel Harris. "Cultural Conflicts in the Writing Center: Expectations and Assumptions of ESL Students" in *The St. Martin's Sourcebook for Writing Tutors*, 3rd ed. Ed. Christina Murphy and Steve Sherwood. Boston: Bedford/St. Martin's, 2008, 211.

about working with you. Take special care to establish a comfortable rapport at the beginning of a session. He or she may worry about an accent or about talking with you in imperfect English. Striking up an informal conversation may help allay fears and calm nerves, and talking easily about the paper may give you some information about the writer's questions and concerns. Even the conversation itself may give you a glimpse of specific difficulties with a second language.

At the same time, be aware that another writer may regard this casual conversation as a waste of valuable time that could—or perhaps should—be spent more directly addressing issues of writing correctly. How to deal? You might try asking something like "We could talk for a few minutes about your paper and writing, and that would help me understand what your concerns are. Would that be OK?"

2. Make an extra effort to put second language writers at ease. In some cultures, asking questions is impolite, so encourage writers to ask questions if they find your comments confusing or unclear.

3. Give directions plainly. Watch writers' expressions, and ask questions to see if they comprehend your explanations. Second language writers may be too embarrassed to admit that they are unsure. They may smile and nod in agreement but still be confused. If you are not sure whether someone understands something, ask him or her to explain what you have said or to give you an example. Be patient and, if necessary, explain again.

4. If a second language writer does not understand a comment or an explanation, rephrase it in different terms. Do not raise your voice or simply repeat the same words.

5. If you have difficulty understanding a second language writer, watch for facial expressions as he or she speaks. The combination of watching and hearing can help you follow what the writer is saying.

6. Many second language writers write better than they speak. Do not assume that because you have trouble understanding someone's speech he or she will have significant problems with writing.

7. Generally, writers should do most, or even all, of the writing in tutoring sessions; however, with some second language writers, handling all the tasks required in a tutoring session—listening, thinking, reading, speaking, writing—can be overwhelming. For example, when writers are exploring ideas for a paper or talking through ways to organize those ideas, the tasks of listening, thinking, and expressing thoughts clearly may be enough for them. It may be helpful for you to serve as scribe, jotting down key words or phrases in the writer's words. At appropriate points, you can use these key phrases to help them start writing or express themselves more clearly. When the session ends, you can hand the student these notes; to reinforce the notions that the paper is the student's own and that he or she, indeed, has ideas and

words to write it, point out that what's on the paper are the student's own expressions and thoughts.

8. Expecting a second language writer to be familiar with English phrases or idioms is sometimes unrealistic. Occasionally, you may need to supply an appropriate word or phrase.

9. Plagiarism is not always the deliberate violation of rules that it seems. In Western cultures, we value originality in writing and regard a piece of writing as belonging to the person who produced it, so we cite the sources of borrowed ideas and words as we write, and we have rules with regard to how to avoid plagiarism. But not all cultures share these values. In some cultures, using another writer's words is a form of flattery, and second language writers may not comprehend the need to document sources clearly. Though you will need to explain Western academic rules and customs about citing sources and doing one's own work, be aware that second language writers may not be knowingly violating those rules.

10. Try not to focus only on the mechanical and grammatical errors in the paper. In second language acquisition, grammatical correctness may take quite a while, and it is only through frequent practice—lots of writing—that a writer will gain proficiency. If you find a grammatical problem that impedes the readability of the paper, point to a couple of places where it occurs and help the writer correct the errors. Then, ask the writer to find similar errors in the paper. This practice will help the writer become independent in his or her own editing.

Tutors tend to believe that they must be expert grammarians to work with second language writers, but that is not necessarily true. As Phyllis Brooks points out, "There is in the tradition of foreign languages and of English as a second language, a long tradition of the native informant: a sympathetic person who is literate and speaks well in his or her own language and can produce correct forms for students to imitate, or can suggest better forms for sentences than the student has tried, unsuccessfully, to produce."[3] Adults acquiring a new language rely heavily on imitation. You can help writers rephrase a sentence and produce other sentences of the same kind. Producing such examples establishes patterns that writers can begin to incorporate into their speaking and writing. You also need to know that you will not be able to explain everything or answer all second language writers' questions about why some phrases or grammatical constructions work in certain ways. Eventually, however, you will become familiar with—and better able to help second language writers correct—some basic kinds of grammatical and syntactical errors.

---

[3]Phyllis Brooks. "Peer Tutoring and the ESL Student" in *Improving Writing Skills: New Directions for College Learning Assistance*. Ed. Thom Hawkins and Phyllis Brooks. San Francisco: Jossey-Bass, 1981, 48.

## The Writer with a Learning Disability

Some writers have problems perceiving or processing information; these cognitive problems interfere with their learning and writing. However, there is disagreement among experts with regard to the causes and treatments of these problems, and only a trained professional can definitively diagnose a learning disability. Even defining the term *learning disability* is difficult and controversial because the symptoms are merely clues: Some are clear-cut, while others are more subtle. Writers with learning disabilities may reverse letters, numbers, and even whole words—for example, seeing or writing *was* for *saw*. They may confuse concepts like up and down. Their handwriting may be difficult to read, and they may misspell words in inconsistent ways. It is important to remember, however, that writers with learning disabilities are not incapable of writing well; they simply process information in ways that can present additional challenges to the writing process.

Coping with a learning disability can be difficult for writers. They may be embarrassed, like the writer who whispers to his tutor that, unlike in high school, he had hoped to make it in college without special assistance and then asks the tutor to help him without letting his teacher know. Or the writer with a learning disability may become easily frustrated and shut down after not understanding a concept following several tries and seek the relief of a quick exit. As a tutor, you need to be especially sensitive to the feelings of these writers. Without being condescending, make them feel comfortable when asking for and receiving help.

Our discussion of learning styles at the beginning of this chapter is especially appropriate for tutoring writers with learning disabilities. They can usually tell you how they learn best and what you can do to make your comments and explanations most beneficial. In many cases, writers are aware of their disabilities and have learned to compensate. They know that they may need to take a test orally or with additional time, for example. If a writer tells you that he or she has a learning disability but does not offer information about coping strategies, ask. Work with these writers as conscientiously as you would with any writer, but take additional care to involve the writer, to structure and sequence material, and then to reinforce that structure. Above all, be patient!

### Some strategies for working with writers with learning disabilities

1. Find a quiet place to work—one that minimizes distractions.

2. Ask what you can do that will best help the writer, both in terms of an approach (perhaps an outline of the paper?) and in terms of tasks (should you, and not the student, do the physical writing?). Teach to a writer's favored learning style. The earlier discussion of learning styles contains specific suggestions to help convey and reinforce information to a variety of people. You might want to be creative and try combining approaches.

3. Be patient, explain things clearly, and repeat or rephrase if necessary.

© Scott and Borgman.

4. As you talk and go through the writer's notes or draft, make lists or outlines or notes that can later serve as guides or reminders for the writer. Toward the end of the session, you might review—and perhaps reorder—them with the writer.

5. Remember that a writer with a learning disability often struggles very hard to accomplish what may come to others quite easily. Support, encouragement, and praise are especially important to a writer who is easily frustrated or discouraged, so take care to offer positive comments liberally where they are due.

6. Be aware that a person with a learning disability may correct something and then immediately repeat the same error. Do not assume that he or she is lazy or has not been paying attention.

## The Adult Learner

Most universities and colleges have an active adult learner population. Sometimes known as the *nontraditional* or *returning* student, the adult learner is a student who is returning to or beginning college several years after high school graduation. Adult learners return to college for a variety of reasons; personal fulfillment, career changes, military discharge, and job promotion are just a few potential motivating factors.

Adult learners typically have spouses, children, jobs, and mortgages and consequently must fit college into an already demanding schedule. Furthermore, because they may not have been in school for many years, they often have considerable anxieties about their scholarly aptitude and performance. Adult learners are often highly motivated; at the same time, they can be extremely demanding of themselves and, by extension, the tutor. Nonetheless, the tutoring session with an adult learner can be most rewarding, as he or she is often extremely attentive and receptive to tutors' advice.

### Some strategies for working with adult learners

1. Be considerate of the adult learner's time. The writer may have taken off work or skipped a daughter's basketball game to come to the writing center, and the writer who submitted a paper electronically to the writing center is likely counting the minutes until you send him or her your advice.

2. Be sensitive to the writer's anxiety and supportive of his or her efforts to return to school despite the obstacles. Maintain an encouraging and empathetic tone.

3. Be aware of age differences and your demeanor. If the person is your elder, he or she may expect you to demonstrate certain signs of respect and may appreciate a more formal tone in the tutoring session.

4. Help writers use real-world experience appropriately in their academic papers. Adult learners come with a vast amount of professional and personal experience, and they frequently like to refer to that experience. Sometimes these references are appropriate and sometimes they are not; you can help them determine when to draw on real-world experiences as evidence or anecdote.

5. Adult learners are often very goal oriented, so setting the agenda and successfully wrapping up and summarizing the session are particularly important. Make sure that the writer has concrete revision plans in place at the end of the session.

6. Do not allow the adult learner to become too dependent on your help. Establish boundaries, and make sure that the writer maintains control over his or her paper at all times. The strategies for "silence and wait time" outlined in Chapter 3 may be very useful. At the close of the session, the writer may resist leaving and might ask for another session with another tutor immediately. You may need to strongly encourage the writer to work on the draft independently and schedule an appointment for another day.

## Exercises for Reflecting on Tutoring Situations

The following exercises ask you to reflect on some of your own experiences as a tutor and as a writer.

### EXERCISE 5A   Reflecting on Writers' Concerns

Think back over your tutoring sessions, and jot down some responses to the following questions.

- What concerns, besides those relating to their assignment, did writers bring with them?

- How did writers express those concerns?
- How did you respond?

## EXERCISE 5B   Reflecting on Your Own Writing Concerns

What concerns have you had over the past year, and how did they affect you as a writer? In what ways can you relate to writers who are learning English as a second language, who have writing anxieties, or who have a learning disability? Is English also your second language, or have you ever tried to learn another language? Have you ever struggled to start an assignment or a task for fear of failure? Have you coped with a learning disability? Have you coped with a disability of another kind—physical or psychological? You might share your thoughts with other tutors and discuss how your experiences influence your role as a writing tutor.

## EXERCISE 5C   Reflecting on Tutoring Techniques

Reflect on your experiences tutoring writers who have writing anxieties or learning disabilities or who are second language writers or adult learners. Make two lists: one of approaches or techniques that you have found especially useful and a second of those that you have found less helpful. Share your lists with other tutors, and discuss why some techniques were more effective than others.

## EXERCISE 5D   Learning from Scholarly Articles

Many educators offer advice on tutoring writers who have writing anxieties or learning disabilities or who are second language writers or adult learners. Find three resources—online or in print—in one of these areas. What suggestions do the authors make? How can you apply them to your own tutoring?

## EXERCISE 5E   Learning from Students

Interview several students from one of the identified areas: those with writing anxiety, second language writers, those with learning disabilities, or adult learners. What can you learn from them about their expectations? What works for them when they write? What doesn't work? Ask them to describe a tutoring session that went particularly well and one that did not. What did the tutor do that helped or hindered? What did they wish the tutor had done or had not done?

# 6

# Tutoring in a Digital Age

The technological options available to writing centers are growing rapidly. Many writing centers offer online tutoring services to help meet the needs of diverse student populations, and now more than ever students are making use of online sources in their research papers. Whether you are a tutor who receives students' papers through an entirely online writing center or one who helps students face-to-face with questions about the validity of online research sources, this chapter will address your special considerations of tutoring in the digital age.

## Online Tutoring

Online tutoring often appeals to both traditional and nontraditional students. Traditional students increasingly expect various components of their college experience to be digital: They register for classes online, renew their library books online, and text their friends between classes. As the number of nontraditional students on campuses increases, nontraditional methods of learning and teaching do so as well. Time and distance no longer restrict learning to a classroom, as students can attend classes virtually. They can also access the writing center from a remote site, which makes tutorial assistance available to many who might otherwise be unable to take advantage of it. From home, work, dorm room, or local coffee shop, writers can access writing center resources, chat with a tutor, or submit their papers electronically for feedback.

Just like the writers who use your writing center, some of you may be excited about tutoring online, while others may be nervous and rather uncomfortable with the technology. Throughout this book, we have addressed tutoring strategies for both face-to-face and online environments, and we have specifically referred to synchronous (real-time) and asynchronous (not real-time) tutoring. Below are a few of the more common forms of synchronous and asynchronous tutoring.

## Tutoring in a Web-Immersive Environment

David Taylor, University of Maryland University College.

## SYNCHRONOUS TUTORING

- **Chat via instant messaging:** Tutor and writer log on at the same time and confer online.

- **Internet phone:** Tutor calls the writer using free Internet phone, such as Skype or iConnecthere, and the two discuss the paper.

- **Video conferencing:** Tutor and writer log on to a Web-based video-conferencing service and chat online, sometimes with a Webcam. Often, the writer can share his or her paper on a whiteboard, a virtual blank space—like a clean piece of paper, a new Word document, or a newly washed chalkboard—on which the writer and tutor can write and share anything they choose. They can just draw and chat on the whiteboard, perhaps exploring the writer's ideas by sketching a clustered diagram or jotting down brainstorming ideas. Or the writer can upload a paper or sections of a paper so they can discuss and comment directly on it.

- **Web-immersive environments:** Tutor and writer meet in an online world, such as Second Life or Sims Online, usually via avatars. The virtual writing center can model the face-to-face writing center, complete with couches, plants, tables, and chairs. The tutor and writer can chat, use a whiteboard, and control the movements of their avatars.

## ASYNCHRONOUS TUTORING

- **E-mail:** Writer e-mails his or her paper to the writing center. Tutors are forwarded papers from a central e-mail server, or they check an e-mail account at appointed times.

- **Database:** Writer submits a paper to an online database. A coordinator or supervisor assigns papers as they come in, and tutors log on to the system and retrieve the papers from an inbox. After the tutor finishes advising the paper, she or he uploads the advice back to the database, where it is then forwarded to the writer.

- **Online classroom:** Tutor facilitates a writing workshop in an online classroom. There may be chat features available, but the majority of conversation is threaded: that is, the writer asks a question and the tutor responds or the tutor posts a topic and discussion question and the writer responds, and so on.

The strategies you use in a face-to-face tutoring session are quite similar to an online session, particularly a synchronous online session, which takes advantage of virtual environments that allow real-time written and oral conversation. A tutor can ask a question; a writer can immediately respond. A writer can compose a thesis statement; a tutor can immediately comment on it. Many whiteboard programs have drawing and reviewing features that can help the tutor accommodate a variety of learning styles. However, if a whiteboard space is cost prohibitive, tutors and writers can still use free synchronous chat features, like instant messaging, to converse about aspects of writing or the paper itself.

Asynchronous tutoring, however, is slightly more challenging because it lacks the immediacy of back-and-forth conversation and thus requires a unique set of strategies, which we will address in this chapter. First, however, let's review four significant advantages of online tutoring.

### 1. Time

For many tutors and writers, the biggest difference between face-to-face and asynchronous online tutoring is the time factor. With face-to-face and synchronous tutoring, writers get immediate feedback. With asynchronous tutoring, however, they must often allow for a turnaround time that can range from a few hours to several days, depending on the writing center's policies and the way incoming papers are monitored. However, this additional time gives the asynchronous tutor more flexibility and means that he or she can potentially go into greater depth with feedback and refine advice. For especially challenging papers, the tutor can take a break and approach the paper refreshed or take the time to ask another tutor for help.

### 2. Collaboration

Many of you may be nervous about losing the collaborative quality of face-to-face tutoring. In synchronous environments, that collaboration can easily be replicated. In asynchronous environments, both tutors and writers may initially miss the physical proximity and immediate rapport that conversation provides, but as you work together you will build a written rapport and may very well come to feel like pen pals. You may also access the writer's previous submissions and advice and refer to them in your comments, thus contributing to an ongoing conversation about his or her writing.

### 3. Anonymity

Because the tutor and writer cannot see one another, the potential intrusion of some stereotypes diminishes. Gender, race, and class become more ambiguous, and shy or socially anxious tutors and writers may feel less inhibited in an online environment.

### 4. Written Record

While the lack of verbal exchange can have disadvantages, writers may gain from having a written copy of a tutor's suggestions. For second language writers, in particular, a face-to-face session can be confusing if a tutor uses idioms or talks quickly; written comments may be more useful because the writer can read them over and over for better understanding or, if necessary, take time to translate them. Writers can print the transcript of a chat session, record a video-conferencing session, and save their asynchronous written advice onto their computers for later retrieval.

### Advice for Asynchronous Tutoring

The asynchronous tutoring session begins much like the face-to-face or synchronous tutoring session, with the writer telling the tutor about the assignment and the specific concerns that he or she has regarding the paper. When writers send papers electronically, they generally identify the course and the assignment then explain what they would like the tutor to concentrate on as he or she reads.

On the other hand, in an asynchronous session tutors cannot use certain signals—like body language and tone of voice—to gauge the writer's level of understanding and the session's progress and to make decisions about how to proceed. Nor can they simply ask the writer clarifying questions and get immediate feedback, as they might if conferring face-to-face or through synchronous chat. Occasionally, this lack of signals may lead to confusion on the part of tutor or writer, but matters can be easily resolved. In an asynchronous session, a tutor often e-mails the writer with brief questions to settle any issues before continuing with the paper. Likewise, writers can use e-mail or chat to request clarification when they receive the tutor's responses.

Asynchronous feedback on a paper should be similar to feedback that you would give in a face-to-face tutorial. Ask questions frequently, and offer statements to indicate that you are responding as a reader. If it is helpful, use a standard form or template created by you or in collaboration with other tutors. A standard template can frame your response to the student as well as ensure a certain consistency in approach and focus. Be sure that your template covers both higher-order and lower-order concerns and allows you to respond to a range of writing issues, from working on the thesis to identifying and correcting comma splices. For an example, see the University of Maryland University College's Effective Writing Center's advice template on page 86.

Just as in face-to-face sessions, the tutor's ultimate focus should remain on helping the student to become a better writer rather than on simply making the piece of writing more effective. Here are some general suggestions for successful online tutoring, followed by specific advice for conducting an asynchronous online tutoring session.

### General Advice for Online Tutors

1. Check e-mail or log on to chat areas at regular intervals so that writers are attended to and papers are assigned in a timely manner.

2. Maintain communication, both with other writing center staff and with writers. Keep your online supervisor or coordinator informed of schedule changes or technological conflicts so that he or she can inform the writer if there will be a delay. If you—the tutor—are the primary point of contact for the writer, keep the writer informed. E-mail the writer to say that you have received the paper and will be in touch soon. If a situation changes, communicate with the writer immediately: "I've been called out of town, but I've given your paper to Yao. You'll be hearing from him this afternoon." Reassurance is important, especially to apprehensive writers, and should be conveyed in writing, not just by voice.

3. If you have access to other technologies, such as audio software, consider embedding audio comments in your advice as well. Audio comments, although still asynchronous, often seem more personal to the writer and appeal to auditory learners.

4. Compile a list of template or stock responses for questions and concepts that come up often, such as "writing a thesis," "effective sentence combining," or "integrating quotations." Written by you or cowritten with other tutors, these templates will save you time. However, keep in mind that you should always personalize these templates to the writer's specific and individual concerns. Remember to revise the templates as you become more familiar and more comfortable with various writing concepts.

The following is an example of stock advice for constructing paragraphs from the University of Maryland University College's Effective Writing Center. Note how the tutor identifies the writing issue, provides a description along with a generic example, applies the stock advice to the writer's specific example, and finally links to additional resources.

### Stock Response for Constructing Paragraphs

How can I develop strong paragraphs? What do I need to include?

✓    Smooth topic sentences with smooth transitional tone.

✓    Body information supporting the topic sentence.

The first sentence in a new paragraph is a topic sentence. This sentence should accomplish two things: It should introduce the new topic and do so with a smooth tone. Adding transition words and rearranging word order can help accomplish this. Here is an example of a smooth topic sentence: "Because of the many roles a working parent has, the first priority includes planning out an organized daily schedule." Do you see how starting with the transition word *because* really helped create a smooth topic sentence? The last sentence of a paragraph should wrap up the main idea before you move on to the next paragraph.

[This is where the tutor applies the stock advice to the writer's paper.]

*Jeremy, your paragraphs are strong and filled with information, but there are times when I am not sure what point you are making. Are you concentrating on the fact that cell phone use is dangerous while driving? Is it that letting your kids distract you is the dangerous thing while driving? Is it that education is the key to learning how to drive safely? I am not certain where your essay is going because you never provided that definite and clear thesis statement. That thesis statement is so important to your essay as a whole. All body paragraphs should support the thesis statement. You will want to keep this in mind as you revise and get your paragraphs to match your thesis.*

What should I avoid when constructing paragraphs?

✗    Eliminate any information not supporting your thesis.

✗    Avoid beginning or ending a paragraph with quoted information.

If you have more questions on paragraphs or transitions, please take advantage of this UMUC audio advice:

UMUC Audio Tutorials: Paragraphs (http://polaris.umuc.edu/ewc/tutorials/paragraphs/)

UMUC Audio Tutorials: Transitions (http://polaris.umuc.edu/ewc/tutorials/transitions/)

#### Points to Keep in Mind for Online Tutoring Sessions

1. Read through the paper completely before making any comments, and think about how the paper works as a whole. As you read, be mindful of any specific questions that the writer may have included with his or her online submission or e-mail and consider whether the paper fulfills the assignment.

2. Watch your time. If your writing center has established time limits for each online session, adhere to them. Generally, you will want to finish

tutoring a paper within one sitting. Try not to take too many or lengthy breaks; they may interrupt your concentration on the paper and make giving advice more difficult.

3. Just as in face-to-face tutoring, use your initial comments to establish rapport and make the writer feel comfortable. Introduce yourself with relevant details, such as your background and the length of time you have been tutoring.

4. Resist the urge to simply edit. For new online tutors working directly with a text, this tendency can be strong. Your purpose is not to proofread, and simply editing the paper actually does the writer a disservice because he or she will not know what to do differently next time. Instead, point out recurring errors, and explain the relevant writing rules.

5. When you identify problematic areas in the paper, always provide examples from the writer's paper as well as an example or a model of a possible resolution. Be specific. Rather than "You need to strengthen your evidence for your second point," write, "I was a bit confused after reading your fifth through seventh paragraphs. You make the following claim, '[quotation from paper],' but I don't see how you back up that claim. Do you have some research that will support this?"

6. Use editing tools cautiously and sparingly and be careful that you do not fall into the trap of editing for the writer. It is more effective to look for significant patterns of writing issues than to simply start at the beginning, marking each "problem" as you read; you can then comment on the patterns you see and the ways to fix or avoid them. Directly marking the writer's paper could be misinterpreted by faculty as plagiarism. It can also suggest to students that only the places you've marked need to be corrected and that they need not look at the rest of their text.

   Some online centers avoid this problem by not allowing embedded comments; they limit tutors' feedback to comments at the beginning or end of the paper. Others allow tutors to embed their comments within the text by placing brackets or asterisks before and after their remarks in order to separate them from the student's text. As a way of modeling, some tutors edit a small portion of the text with explanations for each change and then suggest that the writer go through the rest of the paper and make similar corrections. If you are not comfortable with embedding your comments within the paper, consider copying and pasting a problematic sentence or two into your advice.

7. Use humor and sarcasm carefully. These don't translate as well in writing as they do face-to-face and can offend writers inadvertently.

8. If you have access to the writer's earlier sessions through e-mails or submissions and advice, refer to them. These comments will remind the writer to take another look at previous advice and will reinforce what you or another tutor advised earlier.

9. Write an encouraging closing note. Praise what is done well and explain why, but do not be too effusive. Your comments should be genuine but still acknowledge that there is work to be done. Remind the writer that the paper is a draft; express your praise with statements such as "For a draft, your paper..." The writer can easily misinterpret "This is a great paper" to mean "You'll get an A."

## Online Writing Resources

In addition to offering almost limitless opportunities for research, the Internet provides access to writing resources both for you and for the students you tutor. These resources are especially convenient if you are tutoring online; however, they can also be valuable in face-to-face tutoring. Your center may also have writing tutorial software for writers to use individually or with your assistance; in face-to-face situations it may sometimes be appropriate to leave writers at the computer to do research, use a tutorial, or compose on their own. While we cannot list all the resources available online, we can offer explanations of the kinds of resources and indicate important points to consider when you work with writers or use these resources yourself. The following is a partial list of online writing resources. (For live links to these resources, visit hackerhandbooks.com/bedhandbook.)

### ONLINE WRITING LABS

Many writing centers have established online writing labs, or OWLs, that offer information about their services, staff, and location as well as access to worksheets, style manuals, and research tools. Many also take advantage of the Web's ability to link to documents at other sites, thus increasing the amount of available material. You can easily find another writing center's OWL by going to the college or university's main Web page and doing a search for *writing center* or *writing lab*.

### ONLINE WRITING GUIDES AND HANDBOOKS

Online writing guides and handbooks differ from OWLs in that OWLs are a compilation of resources, and online writing guides offer a single, comprehensive resource. Typically, online writing guides are more linear in format; many even have chapters. For example, the companion Web site for *The Bedford Handbook* (http://hackerhandbooks.com/bedhandbook/) offers a variety of online resources, including writing exercises, grammar exercises, research exercises, and model papers. The exercises are interactive, with explanatory comments and suggestions. The site also includes handouts and other resources for tutors and for students using the writing center.

## ONLINE VIDEOS

Many writing centers develop and post videos online to augment training and to share writing resources. Online tutor-training videos provide a full sense of the tutorial, including both nonverbal and verbal communication, and offer examples of a variety of types of tutoring. Many writing centers also create and share online videos on a variety of writing issues.

## Helping Writers Evaluate Online Sources

In addition to tutoring having a place online, researching and writing have evolved into processes that are often conducted there as well. Most print resources, such as journals and books, go through a review or filtering process, like editing or peer review (a draft of this book, for example, was read by several people who offered comments and suggestions for revision). Information on the Internet, however, is sometimes unfiltered. In essence, the Web can be a kind of vanity press; almost anyone can publish on it, and some resources are not verified by traditional publishers, editors, or reviewers.

Sometimes, a student writer will express confusion over how to find and cite credible Web resources. In such cases, consider modeling online research for the student. As a tutor, it is important that you know the criteria for evaluating information found on the Web as you help guide writers conducting online research for their assignments.

The three main elements of a Web document are its header, its body, and its footer (see the example "Web Page Elements" on page 83). By looking at these components, you should be able to determine the following information, which can then be used to evaluate the document:

- author or contact person (usually found in the footer)
- institution, organization, or company (usually found in either the header or footer)
- date of creation or last revision (usually found in the footer)
- intended audience (determined by examining the body)
- intended purpose of the document (determined by examining the body)
- link to local home page (usually found in the header or footer)

Writers need to consider the authority, accuracy, bias, and currency of any information—whether in print, on film, or online. What follows are some suggestions for helping writers to determine these criteria when they use Internet sources.

## Web Page Elements

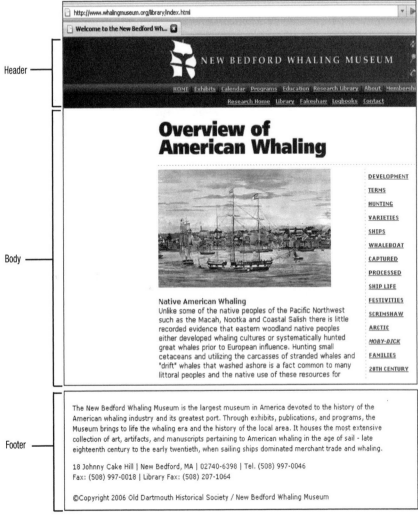

New Bedford Whaling Museum. "Overview of American Whaling" screen shot with footer insert.
© 2006 Old Dartmouth Historical Society/New Bedford Whaling Museum. www.whalingmuseum
.org/library/index.html. Courtesy of the New Bedford Whaling Museum. Reprinted by permission.

## Authority

With any material, you need to determine both the author of the text and the basis of authority from which the author speaks. Because anyone can publish on the Web, it is sometimes difficult to determine authorship of a document, and frequently a person's qualifications for speaking on a topic are absent or questionable. If you do not recognize the author as being well-known and respected in the field, here are some possible ways to determine authority:

- Did you find the address for or link to the author's document from another reliable document?

- Does the document give substantive biographical information about the author so that you can evaluate his or her credentials, or can you get this information by following a link to another document?

- Is the author referenced or mentioned positively by another author or organization whose authority you trust?

If the publisher or sponsor is an organization, you may generally assume that the document meets the standards and aims of the group. You may want to consider the following:

- Is this organization suitable to address this topic?

- Is this organization recognized and respected in the field?

- What relationship does the author have to the publisher or sponsor— does the document tell you something about the author's expertise or qualifications?

### Accuracy

You may be reading information presented by an author or organization unfamiliar to you and need to verify accuracy. Criteria for evaluating accuracy might include the following:

- Are the sources that the document relies on linked or included in a bibliography?

- Is the background information verified? Or, can it be verified?

- Is the methodology appropriate for the topic?

- If the online document is a research project, does the data that was gathered include explanations of research methods and interpretations?

- Is the site modified or updated regularly?

### Bias

To determine bias, remember that any responsible author situates his or her work within a context. Since this context reveals what the author knows about the subject as well as his or her stance on the topic, check the following:

- Was the site developed by a recognized academic institution, government agency, or national, international, or commercial organization with an established reputation in the subject area?

- Does the author show knowledge of theories, techniques, or schools of thought that usually are related to the topic?

- Does the author show knowledge of related sources and attribute them properly?

- Does the author discuss the value and limitations of the approach if it is new?

- Does the author acknowledge that the subject matter itself or his or her treatment of it is controversial if you know that to be the case?

### Currency

Information on some subjects will change rapidly, while for others, it may not change at all. For historical topics like the Civil War, older articles may still be quite useful and valuable. For more contemporary topics related to science or technology, however, currency may be extremely important. You will need to consider the following when examining the document:

- Does it mention dates of publication, most recent update, or copyright?

- Does it give dates showing when information was gathered?

- Does it give information about new material when appropriate?

## Exercises for Tutoring in a Digital Age

### EXERCISE 6A Developing Advice Templates

Review the standardized template on page 86. What are its strengths? What are its weaknesses? By yourself or working with other tutors in your writing center, develop an advice template for your writing center. Try it out in a peer review session in class, or make arrangements to use it reviewing a student's paper.

### EXERCISE 6B The Challenges of Online Tutoring

Consider an activity that you used to perform mostly face-to-face but that you now do online, like shopping, banking, library research, or game playing. Think about mediums of communication, like phone calls and letters, that are now frequently conducted online. What has been lost and/or gained in this transition?

As a student, have you taken courses both face-to-face and online? If so, what were the significant differences? What were the advantages and disadvantages of each approach? Which did you prefer and why?

Bearing in mind your answers to the questions above, what do you think are the unique challenges and opportunities of online tutoring?

### EXERCISE 6C Creating Stock Responses

Identify three or four writing issues that you often encounter as you work with writers. Try to think of both global and sentence-level issues; then write stock responses for each of these issues. For an example, see the stock response for constructing paragraphs on page 79 of this chapter.

## Standardized Template

Tutors at the University of Maryland University College's completely online writing center use a standardized template when replying to student drafts. The template is structured so that major elements (content, organization, and paragraph skills) are treated before sentence-level concerns. The template is divided into the following sections:

- **Salutation.** In addition to greeting the student by name to establish connection and rapport, tutors also use this opening section to offer compliments and encouragement, setting a positive and supportive tone from the very beginning. All tutors include a video welcome message that is also transcribed into the advice.

- **Advice Overview.** This section appears verbatim in each template and explains writing center policies.

- **Assignment Requirements.** Here the tutor compares the assignment requirements to what the student has submitted. Some tutors use a table in this section that lists (1) each assignment requirement; (2) what the student has provided for that requirement; (3) what is needed, if anything, to fulfill the requirements. The tutor reads through the paper first before addressing this section.

- **Thesis & Organization.** Tutors comment on the overall focus and arrangement, including introductory paragraphs and the use of headings.

- **Development & Research.** Tutors comment on the use of supportive material in the body section's paragraphs—their development, unity, and coherence.

- **Formatting & Citations.** Tutors comment on manuscript formatting, documentation, and the use of a style sheet (if applicable).

- **Grammar & Mechanics.** Tutors comment on grammar, punctuation, and usage concerns.

- **Summary.** Tutors provide a numbered list of action items for the student; this list summarizes the tutor's suggestions for improvement.

- **Writing Advisor Info.** Tutors list only their names and the contact information for the writing center. They do not list any personal contact information.

- **More Resources.** Tutors list the URLs of the links provided throughout the template in addition to the writing center's Web site.

For each section, the tutor identifies a writing issue or two, defines that issue, copies and pastes a representative portion from the writer's paper into the template, and offers feedback, sometimes modeling a correction. The tutor also provides links to other online resources. When appropriate, the tutor embeds audio and/or video comments and resources as well. For a more detailed example of an advice template from an online tutor at the University of Maryland University College's Effective Writing Center, visit hackerhandbooks.com/bedhandbook.

# 7

# Helping Writers across the Curriculum

Most schools encourage writing across the curriculum—that is, papers are assigned not only in English classes but also in biology, psychology, engineering, and other classes. You will probably tutor papers from a variety of disciplines, some of which are unfamiliar; however, even if you are not an expert on the topic of a paper, you can still help the writer. Tutors often help writers with papers on subjects about which they have no knowledge, such as the benefits of shale for a geology paper or the treatment of knee injuries for a sports-medicine paper. Tutors also help writers with literature papers about works they have never read.

Regardless of a paper's topic, you can determine whether the ideas are presented in a cohesive and persuasive manner. You can look at larger issues—like organization, style, and tone—or at smaller issues—like grammar and mechanics—and determine whether the writing is effective.

It is also helpful to know about conventions for particular kinds of papers, like lab reports or résumés, so that you can ask specific questions to ensure that the assignment is done effectively. Be aware of various citation styles and distinctions among different fields. If you are unfamiliar with the conventions of the kinds of papers discussed here, check your writing center's print and online resources—writing guides and handbooks, handouts, other information that may be on file, and Web sites. When possible, use the assignment description as a resource. If questions still arise, suggest that the student check with the instructor.

## Research Papers

The research paper is a common genre of academic writing, and you will undoubtedly tutor many authors of such in the writing center. To write an effective research paper, the writer will need to conduct research, interpret that research, and compose a paper that synthesizes both the writer's and

© United Features Syndicate, Inc.

the experts' views of the topic. Proper documentation of evidence is particularly important in research papers; writers may need help selecting appropriate resources to substantiate their claims, integrating information and quotations into their papers, and citing sources within their papers and in their bibliographies.

**A CHECKLIST FOR RESEARCH PAPERS**

☐ If there is a title, is it informative and appropriate?

☐ Is the thesis clear? Is the organization logical? If headings and subheadings are used, do they consistently follow an accepted format?

☐ Are sentences varied in length and structure?

☐ Are tone, voice, and diction consistent and appropriate?

☐ Are transitions smooth from sentence to sentence, paragraph to paragraph, section to section?

☐ Are credible sources and evidence used? Is the supporting material suitable and persuasive? Does it adequately support the thesis?

☐ Are quotations and paraphrased and summarized passages properly introduced with a signal phrase?

☐ Are visual materials—tables, figures, charts, maps, and the like—introduced before they appear in the text?

☐ Are long quotations set off from the text?

☐ Is proper credit given to sources throughout?

☐ Does the paper consistently adhere to the style used (MLA, APA, *Chicago*, CSE, and so on) in format and in documentation, both within the text and in the reference list or list of works cited?

☐ Were the instructions for the assignment—length, number and kinds of resources to be used, directions for title page or documentation—followed carefully?

## Lab Reports and Scientific Papers

Lab reports and scientific papers document the results of scientific experimentation and communicate its significance. Typically, lab reports and scientific papers contain the following sections: title page, abstract, introduction, materials and methods, results, discussion, and references. The *title page* includes the name of the experiment, the participating lab partners, and the date; the *abstract* summarizes the purpose, findings, and conclusions of the experiment; the *introduction* contains a statement of objectives and background information; the *materials and methods* provide the list of materials and the procedure (in chronological, narrative format) used for the experiment; the *results* contain the major findings of the study, including calculations and data; the *discussion* includes interpretation and analysis of the data; and the *reference* section lists full citations for all references cited. Lab reports and scientific papers may also contain acknowledgments and appendices.

The major difference between lab reports and scientific papers is that lab reports are shorter documents whose audience is typically a teacher and classmates. A scientific paper contains the same sections as a lab report; however, beyond presenting and interpreting the experiment, it also puts the experiment in conversation with other research in the field and invites further study. Its audience, therefore, is the scientific community at large.

### A CHECKLIST FOR LAB REPORTS AND SCIENTIFIC PAPERS

☐ Is the title concise, and does it adequately describe the contents? For example, with the title "Substance Y Alters Blonial Structure of Elephant Bone Marrow," researchers interested in substance Y, blonial structures, elephants, or bone marrow will recognize that the article may be of interest to them.

☐ Are the appropriate headings and subheadings included and in proper order?

☐ Are the tone and style appropriate? Scientific writing, for the most part, is intended to be more factual than entertaining and is not embellished with descriptive language, anecdotes, personal opinion, humor, or dialogue.

☐ Does the writer use passive voice, which is the generally accepted convention? The writer of a lab report, for example, should use the passive past tense: "Solution A was centrifuged," not "I centrifuged Solution A."

☐ Is past tense used for describing the procedures and present tense for describing the results and conclusions?

☐ Are sentences short and to the point, expressing facts clearly and concisely? Does the writer answer all basic questions about the topic?

☐ Have conventions related to symbols and abbreviations been observed?

☐ Are figures and tables numbered and accompanied by explanatory captions? Are they introduced before they appear in the text?

## Argument or Position Papers

In argument or position papers, writers take stands on debatable issues, such as comprehensive examinations for graduation, required curfews for teenagers, or the causes of global climate changes. Such papers aim to get readers to think differently about a particular issue or to persuade them to take a certain stance. Writers of argument or position papers should envision skeptical audiences and build arguments that are strong enough to stand up to opponents' views. As they write, they should anticipate readers' objections, refuting them or conceding points while indicating, for example, that there are more important issues to be considered.

**A CHECKLIST FOR ARGUMENT/POSITION PAPERS**

☐  Is the claim or proposition—what the writer is trying to prove—clearly stated?

☐  Are all assertions supported by evidence?

☐  Is the evidence—facts, interpretations of facts, opinions—appropriate? Data should be accurate, recent, and sufficient. Cited sources should be reliable.

☐  Does the arrangement of evidence make sense? Does it emphasize the most important issues? Are there more effective ways of arranging the evidence?

☐  Are facts, statistics, examples, anecdotes, and expert opinions placed properly? Are they used in the appropriate context?

☐  Is the evidence carefully documented?

☐  Is the reasoning sound?

☐  Has the writer avoided all logical fallacies? (If you are unfamiliar with logical fallacies, refer to a writing textbook or handbook.)

☐  Are terms that might be controversial or ambiguous adequately defined?

☐  Have opposing arguments been considered and dealt with adequately?

## Literature Papers

A literature paper analyzes, interprets, or evaluates a text, answering such questions as "What is the significance of the three scaffold scenes in *The Scarlet Letter*?" "What does the cherry orchard in Anton Chekhov's *The Cherry Orchard* represent?" "What is the significance of the setting in John Steinbeck's 'The Chrysanthemums'?" "How effective is the use of first-person narrative in John Updike's 'A & P'?" The writer of a literary essay should answer such questions with a meaningful and persuasive analysis that supports ideas and assertions with specific evidence from the text.

**A CHECKLIST FOR LITERATURE PAPERS**

☐ Is the thesis clearly stated? Is the organization logical and easy to follow?

☐ Does the writer use examples from the text to convincingly support his or her interpretation or analysis?

☐ Has the writer avoided giving a simple plot summary?

☐ Are parts of a work clearly and accurately indicated? Writers need to refer to parts specifically—for example, "the scene in which..." or "at the end of Chapter 3."

☐ Does the writer use the present tense when describing events in a work of literature, as is the convention? (This practice often confuses students. You might explain that the author is communicating to a present reader in the present time.)

☐ Are titles properly punctuated? Titles of short stories, essays, and most poems appear in quotation marks; titles of books, plays, epics, or other long poems are italicized or underlined.

☐ Has the writer referred to the author properly, using the full name initially and the last name in subsequent references?

☐ Is quoted material properly punctuated, indented (if longer than four typed lines of prose or three lines of verse), and documented according to the format specified by the teacher?

# Book, Film, and Play Reviews

A review describes and evaluates a book, film, or production of a play. Those published in newspapers and other periodicals help readers decide whether they wish to read a book or see a movie or play. They assume that readers are unfamiliar with the work and thus offer more summary than an analytical piece might. In reviewing a work, the writer often describes the criteria of evaluation and offers evidence (quotations, examples, and specific references) to support his or her opinions. Though reviews cannot deal with every aspect of a work, they should focus on several; for example, a play review might discuss acting, sets, costumes, lighting, and music in addition to the play itself. A review commonly addresses the purpose, idea, or theme embodied in a work, often in relation to other similar works, and judges its quality by pointing out both strengths and weaknesses.

**A CHECKLIST FOR BOOK, FILM, AND PLAY REVIEWS**

☐ Does the first paragraph include the title and other important information, such as the author's, playwright's, or director's name?

☐ Does the introduction give readers an idea of the nature and scope of the work? Does it establish criteria for evaluation?

❐   Are evaluative terms or phrases, such as "good action" or "like a soap opera," defined? (What are the characteristics of good action or soap operas? How does the work embody those characteristics?)

❐   Does an early paragraph orient the reader by briefly summarizing the plot or contents?

❐   Does the review make reasonable assertions and present convincing evidence (quotes, examples, and specific references) to support those assertions?

❐   Is the tone appropriate? Does it suggest that the reviewer is being fair? Does it indicate respect for readers?

❐   Does the reviewer avoid overuse of phrases like "I think" and "in my opinion"? (Such qualifiers may weaken his or her assertions.)

## PowerPoint Presentations

A PowerPoint presentation facilitates an oral presentation that gives information, explores research, teaches concepts, or proposes a course of action. It offers visual guidelines that outline information as well as reinforce key terms and concepts. These guidelines may include pictures, video clips, or other visual aids that illustrate or highlight points made in the presentation.

Because templates make it easy to create PowerPoint presentations, some writers do so without carefully considering their audience, purpose, or ethos (their credibility or authority in the eyes of the audience). They may crowd each slide with information, expecting it to *be* the presentation rather than to facilitate it. Or, they may get carried away and load the presentation with visuals, so that the audience pays more attention to the glitz than to the presenter's ideas.

### A CHECKLIST FOR POWERPOINT PRESENTATIONS

❐   Has the writer carefully considered the audience, purpose, and occasion for the presentation?

❐   Has the writer carefully considered his or her position in relation to the audience and how he or she wishes to be perceived by them (ethos)?

Sally Forth © King Features Syndicate.

❏   Does the presentation truly complement the talk?

❏   Is the slide progression logical? Is the text simple and phrased in a consistent manner (parallelism)?

❏   If appropriate, does the presentation reinforce key concepts or phrases?

❏   Do the text, images, tables, and graphs, and other visual aids facilitate and complement the presentation?

❏   Does white space appropriately set off text, images, tables, graphs, and other visual aids?

❏   Are the background, colors, fonts, and themes appropriate and consistent?

## Résumés (Traditional)

The résumé and cover letter are designed to get a job interview, not to secure a job as some writers believe. The résumé used to simply offer a prospective employer a quick look at an applicant's educational and work history and provide other pertinent information, such as special skills, awards, and interests. It now also serves as a marketing tool for the applicant, highlighting relevant skills and successful work and education experiences and achievements. Nonetheless, it should be succinct and clear so that prospective employers can absorb information at a glance. (Keep in mind that the résumé you are helping with may be one of hundreds that an employer has to read.)

While composing their résumés, writers often downplay work experience that they think is irrelevant to the job that they are seeking. They assume, for example, that being a bartender or server in a restaurant has little or no relevance to a marketing position. What they do not realize is that the personnel manager of a marketing firm might be impressed by the fact that an applicant spent three years with the same restaurant, won the Employee of the Month award, or had responsibilities for handling money or training new employees. Writers should consider how seemingly irrelevant experience might relate to certain aspects of a particular job and play up those relations in their résumés and cover letters.

## A CHECKLIST FOR RÉSUMÉS

❏   Is the résumé pleasing to the eye? It should be balanced, not crowded at the top or off to one side.

❏   Is all necessary information included? (Check for the student's name, address, telephone number, and e-mail address. Review and ask questions about education, professional or related experience, and other experience.) References are not usually listed unless requested. Sometimes, résumés include a line indicating that references will be furnished upon request.

❏   Is the e-mail address appropriate for a prospective employer? It should contain the applicant's name and not be cavalier or suggestive.

❏   Has the writer eliminated all unnecessary information (such as gender, marital status, number of children, political or religious affiliation)?

❏   Are the parts logically and effectively arranged?

❏   Is the length appropriate? Unless there is a good reason, a résumé should generally be no longer than one page and certainly no longer than two pages.

❏   If an objective is included, is it accurate? (As a professional or career objective, students sometimes write that they seek "an entry-level position as a...," but an entry-level position is an immediate objective, not a long-term goal. Applicants should focus on how the job fits into their career goals, not just their short-term job goals.)

❏   If a summary statement is included, would it catch the prospective employer's eye and begin to answer the question, "What can this person do for me/my company?" Does it succinctly showcase qualifications, strengths, and accomplishments, highlighting specific areas of expertise and the applicant's commitment to them?

❏   Are education and work history (and other such information) in reverse chronological order, with most recent activities listed first?

❏   Has the writer considered all relevant experience, such as volunteer work, internships, course work, and school projects?

❏   Are job descriptions unnecessarily wordy? (For example, phrases like "responsible for" can often be omitted or tightened.) Furthermore, has the writer emphasized his or her strengths without exaggerating or misleading the reader?

❏   In lists, are all the items in parallel grammatical form? (For example, the list "writing proposals, trained new employees, planned staff meetings, Employee of the Year" is not parallel. A parallel version is "wrote proposals, trained new employees, planned staff meetings, earned Employee of the Year award.")

❏   Is the résumé error free? Misspellings, grammatical mistakes, and other errors may cause employers to ask, "If this person is careless in writing a résumé, what kind of work can I expect from him or her?"

"VERY impressive resume, Mr. Miller!"

## Résumés (Scannable)

To sort through and store numbers of résumés, many employers use optical character recognition (OCR) technology, which searches for keywords. These words are nouns and sometimes adjectives that describe specific skills. While some are general—like *leadership, communication,* or *entrepreneurial*—most are specific to particular occupations, industries, and positions. For example, a list of keywords for a position as a social worker might contain *clinical experience, family services, crisis intervention,* and *LCSW.* For an accountant, the list could include terms like *CPA, G/L experience, public accounting,* and names of specific accounting computer programs. Keywords should be incorporated throughout the résumé and punctuation should be avoided as much as possible; the computer might not recognize a keyword if a comma or period immediately follows it. A keyword summary may also be placed at the end of the résumé.

### A CHECKLIST FOR SCANNABLE RÉSUMÉS

❑ Do keywords define education, experience, and skills? Has the writer effectively turned verbs into nouns when appropriate—for example, *designing* into *design specialist* or *coordinating* into *project coordinator*?

❐    Has the writer used common abbreviations, acronyms, and jargon specific to the field, like *BA* for *bachelor of arts*, or *CAD* for *computer-assisted design*?

❐    Is the résumé left justified on standard 8 1/2" x 11" paper?

❐    Is the font a standard typeface? Is the size 10 or 12 points?

❐    Has punctuation been avoided as much as possible?

❐    Is there white space between words and letters (letters must not touch one another)?

❐    Has the writer avoided using italics, underlining, and special characters like bullets?

❐    Has the writer avoided using graphics, shading, boxes, and horizontal and vertical lines?

## Cover Letters

Writers should know that a résumé must always be accompanied by a cover letter. In these letters, applicants should clearly indicate the position being sought, mention how they learned about it (in a newspaper ad, through another person, and so on), and explain how their qualifications suit each requirement listed in the job description. Finally, they should request an interview.

### A CHECKLIST FOR COVER LETTERS

❐    Does the letter follow an acceptable format for a business letter? (See a Web site or a handbook for a discussion of business-letter formats.)

❐    Is the letter addressed to a person rather than to a position? ("Dear Ms. Plotnic" is preferable to "Dear Personnel Manager.")

❐    Does the first paragraph specifically identify the position being sought?

❐    Does the letter indicate how the student learned about the position?

❐    Does the letter acknowledge all requirements mentioned in the ad or job description?

❐    Does the applicant talk in terms of what he or she can do for the employer rather than the other way around? (With the exception of those applying for internships, which are set up to help people learn and gain hands-on experience, applicants are assumed to bring knowledge or expertise to a position; therefore, statements like "I expect to increase my knowledge about the accounting field" are out of place.)

❐    Is the letter error free?

**The bane of every college applicant:
the admissions essay.**

## Essays of Application

Writers often ask for help with essays of application for undergraduate or graduate programs as well as other programs. Though you will need to consider the usual aspects of an essay—organization, tone, and grammar—you need to keep a number of other specific points in mind.

### A CHECKLIST FOR ESSAYS OF APPLICATION

❐  Does the writer establish the point of the essay early on? Is the relevance of the information clearly established? Avoid the mistake made by one applicant, who wrote a lengthy essay describing her harrowing escape from her homeland. Though her point was that if she could withstand those rigors she could manage medical school, she confused readers by waiting until the end to tell them her reason for relating her story.

❐  Does the introduction engage the reader? Does it avoid trite statements like "Ever since I was four and put bandages on my doll, I have wanted to be a doctor"? How will this essay fare against the many others that are being read? A note of caution: Readers want to see how an applicant differs from other applicants, but they can quickly spot outrageous or excessive statements. The writer needs to consider the readers of the application—who they are and what they might be looking for.

☐ On a related point, does the essay sound sincere and honest, or has the writer exaggerated? (For example, becoming a teacher to "change the world" is clearly beyond one person's capabilities.)

☐ Has the writer completely answered the question being posed? Some applications simply ask why one has chosen a particular career or program. Others ask applicants to discuss their strengths and weaknesses, ethics, work experience, accomplishments, or extracurricular activities.

☐ Has the writer included sufficient evidence—often anecdotal—with details that show rather than tell? (For example, rather than write "I am a caring person," the applicant should describe deeds he or she has done that demonstrate caring.)

☐ Has the writer appropriately eliminated extraneous details that do not contribute anything to the essay? (For example, Aunt Mary's illness may have led the writer to consider becoming a doctor. Unless there is good reason, however, readers do not need to know what Aunt Mary prefers for breakfast or the kind of car she drives.)

☐ Does the writer use positive statements and subordination to downplay negative points? A student who received Bs while studying abroad deftly demonstrated this tactic on a law school application by explaining, "When I studied in Spain, I took all courses in Spanish, knowing that doing so would significantly improve my facility with the language, but also likely lower my grade point average."

☐ Is the essay error free? Misspellings, grammatical errors, and other mechanical problems may cause readers to question an applicant's attention to detail.

# 8

# Coping with Different Tutoring Situations

Writers do not bring just their papers to the writing center; they often also bring anxieties, stress, and other personal issues. Thus, you will occasionally encounter some troublesome—or perhaps even difficult—situations while tutoring. A writer who has writing anxiety may come at the last minute, desperate for help. Or, a writer may come only at the insistence of a teacher and be difficult to work with. This chapter offers some specific guidelines for dealing with situations like these. As you work with writers, you will begin to develop your own repertoire of strategies for dealing with uncomfortable tutoring sessions.

## The Writer Who Comes at the Last Minute

You will sometimes encounter a writer who comes in for help just before his or her paper is due. Perhaps the paper is due in two hours and the writer has only an incomplete draft with significant problems. Or, the paper is due tomorrow morning and the writer has no clue how to begin. Such writers may come to you in a guilty panic. How do you handle them?

**DO**

✓ Be kind and sympathetic. Help the writer sort through options and figure out what he or she can reasonably do in the time remaining.

✓ Help the writer consider other options. If it is not possible to complete an acceptable paper by the deadline, is receiving an extension an option? Is there a penalty for turning in a late paper?

✓ Help the writer set goals for future papers. When is the next paper due? Can the writer come in with an outline or a draft a week prior to the due date?

© 1980 United Features Syndicate, Inc.

**DON'T**

✗   Scold or lecture the writer about the need to write papers in a timely manner; you may mean well, but the writer already knows what he or she has done wrong. At this point the writer needs to think clearly and, with your help, figure out the best way to cope with the situation.

## The Unresponsive Writer

Teachers sometimes require students to visit the writing center, and occasionally, such writers come with an attitude of resistance. They may refuse to answer your questions, give halfhearted answers, or otherwise indicate that they do not wish to be there. Often, even their body language is telling. They may slump in their seats, avoid eye contact, or avoid facing you. How do you help these writers?

**DO**

✓   Be patient and polite.

✓   Remind the writer that you are there to help and that the suggestions you offer are just that—suggestions that he or she may choose to accept or reject.

✓   Try to make the tutoring session short but helpful. If you can improve one aspect of a resistant writer's paper, perhaps he or she will see that coming to the writing center is not a waste of time.

✓   Engage the writer as much as possible. For example, have the writer read the paper aloud.

✓   Recognize that even your best efforts may not change writers' attitudes, at least in the initial tutoring session. With hindsight, resistant writers may realize that getting help with a paper is not altogether unpleasant. Another day, they may return of their own volition.

**DON'T**

✗   Lecture writers about your role or their unresponsiveness.

✗   Lose your cool and become angry.

✗   Become unresponsive as well. Try to keep the upper hand in this situation.

# The Antagonistic Writer

For some writers, composing a paper looms as an extremely frustrating—perhaps even impossible—task. They may be apprehensive about writing in general or upset about demands placed on them by a particular assignment or teacher. Often, they view meeting these demands as being beyond their control. If someone could only tell them exactly how to "fix" things, all would be well. Finding themselves in an impossible position, these writers may become verbally aggressive, redirecting their anger and frustration at you or they may show little interest in the suggestions that you offer.

**DO**

✓ Be patient, polite, and supportive.

✓ Allow writers to vent their feelings and tell you what is upsetting them.

✓ Acknowledge writers' anger and frustration with an *I* statement like "I hear how frustrated you are."

✓ Using an *I* statement, rephrase what writers are saying in order to help identify their emotions and problems. You might say, for example, "What I'm hearing is that you're discouraged because you can't figure out how to begin this paper."

✓ If noises or other distractions are interfering with the session, move to a quieter place.

✓ If writers become verbally aggressive, politely tell them that you are not willing to accept such behavior, but do so using an *I* statement. You might say, "When you yell at me that way, I find it difficult [impossible] to listen."

✓ Remind writers that you are there to help and that the suggestions you offer are just that—suggestions that they may choose to accept or reject.

**DON'T**

✗ Lecture students about your role or their behavior.

✗ Get into an argument or a shouting match.

✗ Become hostile or punitive with statements like "You can't talk to me like that!"

✗ Look away and refuse to deal with the situation.

✗ Agree with their judgments and criticisms of assignments, teachers, and grades. Remember that doing so would be unprofessional.

## The Writer Who Selects an Inappropriate Topic or Uses Offensive Language

Occasionally, you may work with writers whose papers are laced inappropriately with offensive language, such as racist or sexist terms. Or you may have difficulty tutoring a paper that takes an extreme and offensive position. What can you do in situations like these?

**DO**

✓ Be patient and polite.

✓ Remind writers that they are writing for an academic community, and ask them to consider how their audience will react to the language or topic.

✓ Respond as a reader and suggest, for example, "Some people might be disturbed by what you say here. I know I am."

✓ Ask the writer to respond as a reader. Ask the writer to identify the audience. Then, say something like "Okay, imagine yourself as a member of your audience. How might you respond to this statement? Are you considering all potential responses to this paper?"

✓ Show writers how to make language more acceptable. You can explain options for avoiding sexist language and suggest alternative terms or ways of rephrasing (many handbooks and guides to writing include sections on avoiding and eliminating sexist language, and you might want to refer students to such discussions).

✓ Occasionally, writers may insist on their right to say what they wish and decline to make any changes. You might suggest to such students that they check with their teacher about the topic (or use of language) before continuing to work on the paper.

**DON'T**

✗ Become angry or hostile.

✗ Take writers' viewpoints or language personally.

✗ Refuse to deal with the situation.

## The Writer Who Plagiarizes

Defining *plagiarism* is difficult at best. Discussions of it often conflate the deliberate use of someone else's work with problems of summarizing, paraphrasing, and documenting sources. On its Web site www.wpacouncil.org, the Council of Writing Program Administrators (WPA) offers the following definition: "In an instructional setting, plagiarism occurs when a writer deliberately uses someone else's language, ideas, or other original (not common-knowledge) material without acknowledging its source." It applies this definition to "texts published in print or on-line, to manuscripts, and to

the work of other student writers." It also distinguishes between deliberate appropriation and the "misuse of sources," explaining that "[a] student who attempts (even if clumsily) to identify and credit his or her source, but who misuses a specific citation format or incorrectly uses quotation marks or other forms of identifying material from other sources, has not plagiarized. Instead, such a student should be considered to have failed to cite and document sources appropriately."

In the writing center, you will likely encounter writers who have committed plagiarism across the spectrum of "intentional" and "unintentional," an issue that may be complicated by people's use of the Web and perceptions of online authorship. Many students are very familiar with Web writing, such as blogs or wikis, and consider such formats "community" writing. In the online world, borrowing language without citation is often considered acceptable. But the culture of authorship online is different from the culture of authorship in academic settings, and you may need to explain this distinction to some writers.

As a tutor, you should become familiar with your institution's code of academic integrity, with its definitions of academic dishonesty, and with the guidelines that it uses to enforce them. At some schools, tutors must report their suspicions of plagiarism; at other schools, tutors may explain what plagiarism is and advise writers to be careful about how they use and document information.

**DO**

✓ Be familiar with your school's academic code of integrity.

✓ Be familiar with your writing center's resources (manuals, handbooks, handouts, online explanations) for properly summarizing, paraphrasing, and documenting information.

✓ Explain the importance of carefully taking notes from sources. Remind writers to indicate the author's words clearly and to gather accurately all information that might be required for a citation.

✓ If you encounter a suspicious passage or phrase, explain that the text sounds "different" or "funny" and seems to be taken from another source. Explain that material taken from another source that is not common knowledge must be documented, whether it is quoted directly, paraphrased, or summarized.

✓ Keep in mind that some writers concentrate on content in early drafts and do not include all information for citing portions of their papers at that stage; they add those details later. Or, an entire class may be responding to the same reading(s), and the teacher may have said that citations are therefore not necessary in this paper. If you are unsure, ask the writer for more information about the citation requirements for that assignment.

✓ Explain that acknowledging sources is an ethical issue, a matter of giving credit for ideas and/or words to the person who came up with them. Documenting sources appropriately both acknowledges the original writer and allows readers to locate that resource easily if so desired. Remember that this policy applies to Web writing as well.

✓ Speak with your director or supervisor if you are unsure about how to handle a suspected case of plagiarism.

**DON'T**

✗ Accuse a writer directly of plagiarism.

## The Writer with the "Perfect" Paper

The "perfect" paper really is not a problem because it does not exist. Even if the paper seems to meet all the criteria for the assignment and the writer has expressed his or her thoughts well, you can still encourage the writer to look for areas that might be improved.

For a paper that is quite strong, some refining at the editing and revision stage can make the paper even more effective. Usually, such refinements amount to tweaking the paper at the sentence level. Furthermore, for some writers, effective writing is more intuitive than conscious. It also may be helpful for the writer to reflect on the strong aspects of the paper. Consciousness of these good writing skills and patterns can then be conveyed to future papers.

On the other hand, you may encounter a writer who is confident that he or she has written the perfect paper and may even announce that fact. Rather than challenge that statement, a good place to start is to praise aspects that appear to be well done, then ease into pointing out places where there is room for improvement. Responding as a reader works well in such instances, for you can note an inviting introduction and good transitional sentences, then identify one or two places where the evidence, sentence structure, or word choice could be even stronger. Once you work through one or two issues, she or he may be more open to the revising process.

**DO**

✓ Ask the writer which areas he or she thinks need more work. Being more familiar with the material and topic of the paper, the writer may know specifically what part needs stronger development.

✓ See what stylistic changes might be made, like combining sentences or shifting a phrase for better emphasis.

✓ Examine vocabulary carefully. Where might a better, more precise word replace an already good word?

✓ Identify and discuss particularly strong passages with the writer.

**DON'T**

✗ Assure the writer that he or she has an excellent paper. High praise may seem to be in order, but it should come from the teacher, not you. Remember that you may be unaware of some aspect of the assignment that may influence the grade.

## The Writer with the Long Paper

You will see a variety of paper topics, genres, and lengths in the writing center. This diversity is part of the fun of tutoring! But it can also be a challenge. The majority of writers you tutor in the writing center will likely bring in papers less than ten pages long. However, occasionally you will encounter a writer with a much longer paper, perhaps a capstone paper or honors thesis. Along with the writer, your task is to identify what the two of you can reasonably accomplish in a session, which usually means focusing on a particular aspect or portion of the paper.

**DO**

✓ Find out if your writing center has a policy on paper length; some writing centers set limits on pages per session, while others ask that writers submit longer papers ahead of time so that consultants can read beforehand.

✓ Ask the writer to prioritize the writing difficulties that she or he is having.

✓ Ask the writer to identify a manageable portion of the paper that may be fairly representative of these writing difficulties.

✓ Suggest that the writer return to the writing center with another section of the paper after she or he has further revised.

**DON'T**

✗ Feel obligated to "get through" the entire paper. This will only force you to rush through the session and potentially overwhelm the writer.

## Exercises for Coping with Different Tutoring Situations

### EXERCISE 8A   Role-Playing Different Tutoring Situations

Read through each of the following three scenarios twice. (If you are using this guide as part of a tutoring class, you and other tutors may want to act out the different parts.) As you do the preliminary read, consider the following questions:

1. How is the tutor probably feeling? How do you know? What verbal and nonverbal clues indicate his or her feelings?

2. How is the writer probably feeling? How do you know? What verbal and nonverbal clues can you find?

As you go through the scenarios the second time, consider the following questions:

1. What are the tutor's expectations?

2. What are the writer's expectations?

3. What are some other ways in which the tutor might have handled the situation?

These scenarios provide excellent material for group discussion, and you can use the preceding questions as departure points.

## SCENARIO 1

*Tutor:* Hi! [Smiles.] My name's Chris. We can just sit over here. Grab that chair. [They sit.] What can I do for you?

*Writer:* Well, I'm Jeremy, and I have this paper [hands it to tutor], and, uh, my teacher said, I had to come here and, uh, get some help 'cause my last paper... [looks down] was a D.

*Tutor:* Then maybe we should just begin by reading through it out loud. Do you want to read, or would you rather I did?

*Writer:* [Motions to tutor and mutters "You," then folds arms across chest and gazes off into space.]

*Tutor:* [Begins reading but is clearly having trouble. Stumbles over words and stops several times to clarify a word. As tutor reads, writer occasionally sighs, taps fingers on desk and feet on floor.] Listen, I'm really having trouble reading your handwriting. It would probably be easier if you read your paper to me. Would you mind?

*Writer:* [Hesitates.] Naw, I guess not. [Reads about halfway down page, suddenly stops and slams hand down on desk and looks at tutor.] I really don't see the point of this.

*Tutor:* Well, it's just easier for me to tutor, to help you with your paper, if I hear what you've written.

*Writer:* [Waits a few moments, then tosses paper in front of tutor and speaks in a demanding way.] Can't you just check it and fix it?

*Tutor:* When you come here and ask to have a paper proofread, the receptionist will tell you that the writing center isn't a proofreading service. It's a tutoring service. You can have a tutor like me look at your paper with you and discuss your problems and then try to show you how to correct them. We don't just correct students' papers!

*Writer:* [Annoyed.] Well, I was told that you did! My friend said I could just have a tutor correct my grammar.

*Tutor:* [Firmly.] Well, I'm sorry. I don't tutor that way. [Silence.]

*Tutor:* If you want me to continue reading through...

*Writer:* [Cuts tutor off, snatches paper away from tutor, looks quickly at watch.] I just don't have time for this. Nothing against you, but I just don't have time for this. [Collects papers quickly and gets up.]

*Tutor:* [Stares in disbelief.] I'm really sorry. I just don't tutor that way.

*Writer:* That's okay. It's nothing against you. [Walks out.]

## SCENARIO 2

[The tutor is sitting at a computer, and a student IMs her for a writing center online chat.]

*Tutor:* Hi! I'm Jomeka. What can I do to help you?

*Writer:* I don't know if you can. I only have a draft of a paper, or the start of one. Not sure what to do. Just wrote some stuff down. Parts of it just don't sound right.

*Tutor:* What's your assignment?

*Writer:* A book review for history. Nothing specific, really, just a review. The book's *Lincoln at Gettysburg*, by Garry Wills.

*Tutor:* ☺ Great! Have you ever written a book review before? Do you know what you're supposed to include?

*Writer:* Sort of. I think I'm supposed to give my opinion.

*Tutor:* Something like that. What you're supposed to do is evaluate it and use evidence from the book—like quotes and examples and references—to back up what you say. So tell me some of your ideas. What did you like about the book? Take your time; I'll be here!

[The cursor blinks for a few minutes.]

*Writer:* Well, I don't really know. Have you read it? What do you think about it?

*Tutor:* Nope, haven't read it. Sorry! Why don't you just tell me some of your ideas. That will be a good starting point.

*Writer:* If you haven't read the book, I don't see how you can help me.

*Tutor:* I understand your frustration! But I think I can still help. In fact, it's probably better that I haven't read it. You'll have to explain things to me, and that'll help you sort out your ideas. If you just tell me what some of your ideas are, we can chat about them and I can help you think them through a bit. I do that all the time here.

*Writer:* I just don't see how that will work. I mean, if you haven't read the book... ☹

*Tutor:* Yes, but you have, so it's really not a problem. I can tell that this is frustrating for you, but I can help.

[The cursor blinks again for a minute or so.]

*Tutor:* You have read the book, haven't you?

*Writer:* Most of it. I mean, it's really long, and I don't know. I can't get into it.

*Tutor:* Well, maybe you could tell me about the parts you have read, and we can at least start working from there. You said you wrote some things down. Can you e-mail me or copy and paste what you do have? It'll be a good start...

**SCENARIO 3**

[The tutor is sitting. The writer sits down beside the tutor.]

*Tutor:* [Cheerfully.] Hi! I'm Lee. What are you working on?

*Writer:* I have to do a five-page paper analyzing this poem. It's due tomorrow morning—early. I don't know. It's really hard to do that stuff, don't you think? Why do teachers give assignments like this, anyway?

*Tutor:* Well, they do. And, I know, sometimes it's just not easy.

*Writer:* [Hesitates.] Uh, I haven't really started it yet. Because I can't figure out what I'm supposed to do. Here's the poem and here's the assignment sheet. [Hands poem and assignment sheet to tutor.] What should I do? I really don't understand what the teacher wants.

*Tutor:* [Glances at papers.] Oh, I know that poem. [Looks up.] Did the teacher explain anything about the paper in class?

*Writer:* Yeah, we're supposed to read the poem and analyze it, but I just don't know what she wants. [Looks baffled.] How do you analyze a poem?

*Tutor:* Well, let's see what the assignment sheet says.

*Writer:* [Sighs.] I can't figure out the assignment sheet. It's so confusing to read. Can you read it and tell me what I'm supposed to do?

*Tutor:* [Hesitates, glances at it, and then smiles.] Sure, let me read it. It's short. [Reads it over.] Oh, here it is! At the bottom it tells you what to do.

*Writer:* Oh, I didn't read that far. I got confused by the beginning stuff, with all those terms. The teacher never really explains anything to us. I hate that.

*Tutor:* Well, let's see if we can sort it out. The poem...

*Writer:* [Interrupts.] Don't you just hate when teachers don't tell you what they want? If they just would tell me, I think I would be able to write it. [Pauses and grins.] So, you figured out the assignment? What am I supposed to do?

*Tutor:* [Pauses.] You know, what I'm hearing is that you're frustrated because you don't know what to do and the paper's due tomorrow. Let's look at the assignment sheet together. You can tell me which parts confuse you, and I can try to explain...

*Writer:* [Angrily.] Look, I have to pass this class and I have to do the paper to pass it. Just tell me what to do! You know the poem and you know what I'm supposed to do...

*Tutor:* [Firmly but politely.] Yes, but I can't do the paper for you. I can help you, but it's your paper.

*Writer:* I know, I know, I know, but what am I supposed to do? It's due tomorrow! [Emphatically.] I hate poetry!

*Tutor:* Well, I'm trying to help, but...

*Writer:* Yeah, but it's so late. Just tell me what to say! Aren't you supposed to help me?

*Tutor:* I can help you, but if you don't want to do your share of the work, there's not much I can do.

*Writer:* [Grabs the papers.] Yeah, well, thanks for nothing. I should have figured you tutors would be just like the teacher.

### EXERCISE 8B   Reflecting on Different Tutoring Situations

Think about a tutoring session in which you were not satisfied with the outcome. What made the situation so unpleasant, both for you and for the writer? How did you handle the situation? What are some other ways you might have handled it? Now think about a tutoring session in which you were satisfied with the outcome. What made the situation pleasant for both you and the writer? What did you learn from this situation and how might it help you navigate future difficult tutoring sessions?

# 9
# Summing It All Up

One of the best things about tutoring is that it is never stagnant. Because different writers come with different assignments and different perspectives, no two sessions are ever the same. Even those who have been tutoring for many years recognize it as a professional activity in which they continue to learn and grow.

As a tutor, you are now engaged in this professional activity. Happily, it is a collaborative and friendly profession, one that welcomes members at all levels—peer, graduate, professional, administrative—and encourages exchanging ideas and learning from one another. It offers arenas for participation at all levels, and we urge you to explore becoming an active member. We have built an annotated bibliography of tutoring resources that is available on the Web at www.hackerhandbooks.com/bedhandbook and can help you in this endeavor.

To begin, check out the Web site for the International Writing Centers Association (IWCA), a National Council of the Teachers of English Assembly: http://writingcenters.org. Consider joining IWCA. A membership gives you important publications:

- *Writing Center Journal* (*WCJ*)*:* Published twice yearly, *WCJ* includes articles on issues and trends of interest to tutors and writing center administrators. It also features a blog.

- *Writing Lab Newsletter* (*WLN*)*:* Published ten times a year, *WLN* features articles also of interest to tutors and writing center administrators and includes a tutor column.

The IWCA Web site offers timely and practical information about writing center work for peer, graduate, and professional tutors as well as for writing center directors. It also links to many important, useful, and interesting Web sites, including online journals, resources for writers, and discussion forums. Chief among them is WCenter, an open, friendly, international discussion group devoted to tutoring and other related issues. The IWCA Web site also connects to discussion groups that focus on issues of particular interest to peer consultants/tutors, graduate students, and high school writing centers.

Through these Web sites and publications, you will learn of the many local, regional, and national meetings and conferences devoted to tutoring writing. All invite tutors not only to attend but also to explore issues and present papers, panels, and workshops.

If you have worked your way through this book while actually tutoring, then you have been gathering your own repertoire of information about writing and helping writers. Whether you interact face-to-face or online, you likely know more about the writing process and have developed a sense of what is comfortable for you as a tutor. You can work—fairly easily, we hope—with writers who have different learning styles, competencies, attitudes, and assignments; you can assess their needs and plan and manage a session, adapting even as dynamics change within a session.

You know what questions to ask and can make suggestions and give writers the tools to tackle their writing projects more confidently and successfully. Whether you tutor for a short time or for years, this repertoire of information will be developed and refined, but already you have begun cultivating your own philosophy of how to tutor effectively. Articulating that philosophy will help you to clarify it and reveal those places where you might want to read, talk, and think more about what it is that you do as a tutor.

The following activities encourage you to consider your role as a writing tutor. The first offers you a formal way to consider it; the second offers a more creative approach. We hope that you will do both and share your thoughts with other tutors.

## Exercises for Developing Your Philosophy of Tutoring

### EXERCISE 9A   Reflecting on Your Tutoring

In a five- to six-page paper, reflect on your tutoring experiences thus far. Your paper should synthesize three areas: your work with writers; book and article readings about composition, tutoring, and writing centers; and your discussions—formal and informal—with other tutors. In determining a thesis and planning your paper, think about the intersections of these areas.

You may choose to write about tutoring in general, or you may focus on a particular issue to which you find yourself returning frequently, like tutoring second language writers or determining the agenda for sessions or underscoring writers' responsibility for their own papers. Or, you might discuss two or three sessions that were especially meaningful to you in light of readings and discussions. What is important is that you synthesize your tutoring experiences with writing center research in order to arrive at your own tutoring philosophy.

## EXERCISE 9B    Creating a Metaphor for Tutoring

From William Shakespeare describing the world as "a stage" in *As You Like It* to Robert Burns declaring that "O my Love's like a red, red rose" ("A Red, Red Rose," 1794) to actress Katharine Hepburn saying she is like an oak tree to a tutor comparing herself with a flight attendant or a pastry chef, people use metaphors to compare unlike entities. Such comparisons range from simply noting a similarity to serving as a central idea and controlling image. The latter—an extended metaphor—often captures the beliefs or assumptions that underlie someone's attitudes or beliefs about the subject.

What follows is John's comparison of tutoring with jazz, one tutor's example of an extended metaphor.

> Tutoring is like playing jazz. Improvisation and good timing are musts for jazz musicians, and the same holds true for tutors. During jazz improvisation periods, band members must be able to alter their style to fit the needs of the song. For example, a bass player must constantly be aware of the drummer's tempo because it could change at any time. If the bass player does not alter his playing to fit the drummer's rhythm then the entire song sounds out of synch. Similarly, as the writer and tutor talk and work with a draft, the writer's needs could change at any time; if the tutor does not adapt to fit those needs then the session may not be as helpful as it could be.
>
> Part of the bass player's responding to the drummer's change in tempo involves adaptability, and it's the same with the tutor's responding to the writer's needs. In both cases, you have to know enough to be able to shift gears, to change your way of approaching the song or of explaining things to the writer, and to do so on the spot.
>
> Although jazz relies heavily on improvisation, all musicians also must be aware of the rules, or theory, of music, which correlates directly with how a tutor must approach a session; the tutor must always be cognizant of the major theories and philosophies of tutoring when working with a writer. These are the matters that play around in the background, but they are a significant and necessary part. Finding an appropriate mix of improvisation and theory is difficult in both jazz and tutoring; however, it is this very challenge that can make both experiences rewarding, pleasing, enjoyable, and successful.

Think of a metaphor that aptly describes tutoring for you or one that characterizes writing and the roles that tutors and writers play in the process. In a paragraph or two, extend that metaphor. Begin by stating that "tutoring is [like] X" and then explain how or why the two are similar. Share and discuss your metaphors with other tutors, and consider ways in which each might be extended even more.

This exercise is also an interesting one to do as a visual representation, using an image or creating a collage of pictures to depict your statement "Tutoring is like..."

As a tutor, you have joined an active, engaged group of professionals. Someone once noted that tutoring writing is one of the few truly professional activities in which a student—whether high school or college—can participate. We hope that you will not only take advantage of all that tutoring has to offer you but also have fun, learn much, and enjoy being part of this community as you do so.

## Tutors Ask...

The following questions were posed by tutors. See what kinds of suggestions you can come up with for dealing with the situations that they describe. If possible, share your ideas with other tutors. (You may use the questions as departure points for group discussion in class or online.)

1. What can I do to make writers do more of the work in a tutoring session? How can I help them discover more of the answers themselves? How do I do this in an online environment?

2. What can I do with papers that seem just fine? I worked with someone the other day, and I just couldn't come up with any real suggestions for improving the paper.

3. I had a writer who was working hard, but she kept talking about how she thought the assignment was just too difficult. I tried to sympathize, but I was afraid she'd think that I agreed with her. What could I have done?

4. What can I do if I don't fully understand the assignment? A writer tried to explain his assignment to me so I could help him get started, but he was so vague, and I couldn't really tell what the teacher was looking for. Online, I had the description of an assignment, but it was only two sentences!

5. What should I do when a lazy writer comes into the writing center assuming that the tutor will come up with all the ideas? I tried so hard to get this particular writer to think and come up with his own ideas, but he just sat there silently or said, "I don't know."

6. What can I do for people who come in ten or fifteen minutes before closing and can't come back the next day? Should I try to help them anyway? How?

7. Should I allow writers to walk out of the writing center with glaring errors still in their papers? What impression will teachers—or even those writers—have of the writing center when that happens?

8. In a session yesterday, I worked with a writer who was quite frustrated with her schoolwork, her assignments, and her professor. What made me most uncomfortable was her attitude toward the professor and his assignments. She seemed to be quite negative from the start. I could

feel the tension. Her body language and facial expressions indicated that she was feeling a great deal of stress. I got her to calm down a bit, and I basically let her air some of the gripes that she had. After letting off some steam, she seemed to feel a bit more relaxed and comfortable. What else can I do to help in this kind of situation? I felt like I spent most of the session just getting her to calm down. Wasn't this a waste of time? Was it worthwhile to have a tutoring session?

9. Some writers just want a quick fix and get impatient when I start explaining why something is wrong. How can I get someone to really listen when I explain these things?

10. A writer submitted a paper to the online writing center and only wrote that she wanted it "proofread." How do I know where to get started?

11. Sometimes a writer leaves with an attitude that suggests that I was of no help whatsoever. When this happens, how much should I blame myself? The writer? What can I do to avoid this kind of problem?

12. As I worked with a writer on a paper, I realized that not all the work was his. He wrote about some things he couldn't explain and used words he couldn't define. What's the best way to deal with a situation like this?

13. I'm taking a literary criticism course from a professor who also teaches a poetry class, and I tutored one of his students from that class the other day. Yesterday the professor stopped me and asked about that session. I had another class, so I couldn't stay to talk, but I felt very uncomfortable being asked about a tutoring session like that. What should I do if that happens again?

14. From a female tutor: A guy came in for help with a paper, but when I began to work with him, all he did was stare at me. He went so far as to compliment my appearance. I couldn't get him to focus on his paper. Pretty soon, I felt so uncomfortable I couldn't focus on his paper either. What could I have done?

15. What should I do if I'm scheduled to tutor someone from a class I'm taking, probably working on the same assignment I'm working on?

16. A student brought a paper that had already been graded. Though she said she wanted me to explain the teacher's comments, it quickly became apparent that she disagreed with the grade and really just wanted me to support her point of view. I think she wanted to be able to go back to the professor and say, "The Writing Center says you're wrong." I did think the professor was rather harsh, but I didn't want to say that to the student. What's a good way to handle a situation like this?

17. A student brought in a take-home exam and wanted help. I wasn't sure if that was something I should do or not. Are there times when it might be okay? Times when it might not be?

18. Several weeks ago, a friend came to my dorm room. She wanted help with a paper because she knows I tutor at the writing center. I was studying for a test, but she was so desperate that I helped her for about an hour. When I saw her yesterday, she was mad because she got only a C on her paper. I gave up my study time and she's mad? How should I have handled this situation?

19. Every so often I get a writer who wants more help than I think I can give. I don't know much about what should be in essays of application for graduate school, for example. I don't want to look stupid, but I don't want to give someone advice that might not be very helpful. What should I do in a case like this?

20. I sometimes tutor students privately. One of them wanted to see me when I finished work at the writing center yesterday. He didn't have much time and wanted to work with me there. It didn't seem right, but I didn't know what to say to him.

21. We have a set time limit for our appointments, but sometimes a writer gets really pushy about wanting more time. How can I deal with a rude person without being rude myself?

22. I think I may have inadvertently offended someone when I was tutoring them in an online chat. I made a little joke, followed by LOL (laugh-out-loud), and then there was just "silence" on the other end. In a face-to-face, I'd know how to recover, but in this situation, I had no idea what I did wrong or how to make it OK.

23. I work with the same writer every few days. Today I learned that she sees other tutors with the same paper between our appointments. I suspect she does little or nothing on her own; instead, she just takes the specific suggestions one tutor makes, then moves on to another tutor. What should I do?

24. Some writers expect me to be an expert on documentation. They ask me really specific questions, like "Should I have a comma or period here?" or "How do I cite a conference paper posted on someone's home page?" They seem to think I'm stupid for not having this information on the tip of my tongue. What do I say to them?

25. A student came with her senior thesis and asked for a "final look through." She was so proud of her paper and seemed to just want praise for it. Unfortunately, her documentation was not only incomplete but also incorrect. I pointed that out in several places, but she insisted she had done everything her teacher had told her to do. What's a good way to handle this kind of "last minute," troublesome situation?

26. A student asked for help with sentence structure in his paper. I did everything right—made sure he did all the writing as I suggested ways to rephrase sentences—but he made me feel as if I were dictating changes to him. He'd say, "That's good; tell me again slowly," and he'd

write down my suggestions word-for-word then move on to the next sentence. What's a good way to handle a situation like this?

27. I helped a student who was really nice and even fun to work with. As we finished the session, he asked for my e-mail address "in case he had more questions." I didn't know if I should give it to him or not.

28. I just started tutoring online and I'm surprised by how much time it takes! I spend two hours at least on each paper. I want to make sure I don't copyedit, but I feel compelled to address every issue.

29. A writer came for help on a research paper. She seemed fine at first—really willing to listen to suggestions—but several minutes into the session, she began to cry and said she just wasn't "good at research." I shared some of my own frustrations about writing but wondered what else I could have said to help her.

30. As I helped a second language writer with his paper, I realized he was thinking in his native language and then attempting to translate his words into English. While his ideas were fine, they got lost as he tried to put English words and phrases on paper. What are some good strategies for a situation like this? Also, am I allowed to provide him with words that he's having trouble finding, especially idioms?

31. I really enjoy tutoring and some of the writers I've worked with seem also to get a lot out of the tutoring session—so much so that a few have begun requesting me rather adamantly. I'm kind of embarrassed, but I also feel like I have a good handle on these writers' particular problems, since I see them often. Then again, some students seem to be getting dependent on me, scheduling multiple appointments ahead of time and making comments like, "We got a B+ on this one" and "I couldn't have done it without you." Is it OK for me to have "regulars"? How should I handle their future requests?

32. I primarily tutor online. A writer submitted a paper that she failed, complete with the professor's in-depth comments explaining why. The writer mentioned that she is having trouble applying these comments to her paper. I am not sure what I can add to the teacher's comments—they seem pretty fair and extensive. Is it even my place to help interpret her professor's comments? Since I only communicate with her asynchronously online, what are some ways that I can appropriately phrase my advice?

33. The writers I work with are often frustrated by the number of rules instructors have about the Internet: You can't use more than five Web sources, they must be "credible," and you can't use Wikipedia. If the Internet is such a great resource, why attach so many rules to it?

# Appendix B

## Tutors Talk: Evaluating What They Say

In each of the following examples, indicate what the tutor said or did that was or was not effective, and explain why. Describe what the tutor might have said or done instead. (You may use the examples as departure points for in-class or online group discussion.)

1. Wow! You have a problem with run-on sentences. Let me get you a worksheet that explains how to fix them and an exercise to practice with. When you finish, let me know and I'll correct it.

2. Hi, I'm Eric. Let's sit down over here. You can put your book bag there and then tell me what you're working on.

3. Help you... now? We usually take people on the hour. I've just tutored two people and I'm tired. Besides, I have an econ exam this afternoon, and I was hoping to get a few minutes to review stuff. How much help do you need?

4. Here, in your paper, you say that "most upper-level courses require research papers." If you really want to convince your audience, you need to support that statement with an example or two. Can you give me one—a specific one?

5. This paper is great! Your teacher's sure to love it. I had Dr. Brunetti last semester, and he likes anything about World War II.

6. I always get confused between restrictive clauses and nonrestrictive clauses, too. I don't want to tell you the wrong thing, so let me get a grammar handbook, and let's check out the rules.

7. You keep saying "I think...," but your teacher already knows that you're writing this paper and that the ideas are yours. Let's take this sentence. How can you rephrase it without using *I think*?

8. Your paper's due tomorrow and these notes are all you have? You should have written at least a draft by now.

9. You have a lot of misspellings and grammar problems. Let me read you this paragraph and show you what happens to me, as a reader, when I have to deal with so many mistakes.

10. You're arguing in support of stem cell research? I don't think I can work with you. I'm against it.

11. It doesn't really matter if English is your second language. You have to fit in—you know, "When in Rome, do as the Romans do."

12. Do I ever sympathize! I used to make this same sort of mistake all the time. Then I learned what conjunctive adverbs are and how they work with semicolons and commas. Let's take this sentence where you use the word *however*, and I'll explain.

13. Why don't I just read your paper, and then I'll tell you what I think.

14. I'm not sure what your point is in this paragraph. Why don't you just tell me what it is you're trying to say?

15. I'm so glad you got me for a tutor. I took that class last semester and I have lots of ideas about that poem.

16. Let me play devil's advocate. You're arguing against fraternities, but I belong to one and there are lots of advantages.

17. You do have a problem if this paper's due this afternoon. Let's see what we can do, but I suggest you ask your teacher for an extension.

18. I'm really just here to help. Anything I tell you is just a suggestion. You can take my advice if you want, but you don't have to.

19. This looks like a really hard assignment. I don't quite understand it either. Professor Cunningham never does explain things very clearly. What do you think you're supposed to do?

20. Look, all you have to do to make this better is put in some more details. Here, when you look out of the window of the plane, talk about how tiny everything is. And with the food, say it tasted bland or delicious or whatever, then when you get to the landing part, say it was bumpy, smooth, loud, quiet, whatever it was. You'll have a good paper then.

21. I'm not an expert on documentation. You have a handbook. Just look it up.

22. I like your paper. It's really solid.

23. So this internship application asks you what you hope to accomplish through participating in it and how it relates to your academic and career goals. But, you know, everyone applying is smart and can benefit from it. So what about you makes it especially relevant? What do you expect to gain? What can you learn? And then, is there anything about your background—your studies and experiences—that might help them?

24. Clearly, you have some article usage problems. Are you ESL?

25. I also just had to write a twelve-page paper last week and thought I'd never finish! Where are you in the process? What do you think you can accomplish in the next three days before it's due?

# Appendix C

## Presenting at a Conference

Because as a tutor you are involved in a professional activity, you may have the opportunity to attend conferences to share ideas and to learn new approaches for dealing with tutoring issues. Many writing center conferences encourage peer tutors to participate, both as attendees and as presenters. Since presenting at a conference for the first time can be intimidating, you might find the following suggestions helpful.

### 1. PLANNING

Most conferences feature a theme. While not all presentations must adhere to that theme, it can be helpful to keep it in mind as you consider possible topics. Your presentation should address a topic or question that you feel writing center research has not already fully explored or answered or one that can benefit from being revisited.

As you think about a topic to present, also keep the audience in mind. Who are they? Are they new or experienced tutors? Are they directors? Writing teachers? You do not want to tell them what they already know; you do want to share your research on a subject, present a new way of looking at a topic, or engage them in a discussion or workshop about handling particular situations or kinds of students. Providing them with questions to answer or scenarios (written, online, videotaped, or acted out) to discuss, for example, means that they will be actively involved in sharing their ideas about and experiences with your topic.

Consider time constraints. What can you reasonably do in the time allotted? In thirty minutes, you could not possibly deal with the topic "difficult tutoring situations," but you could select one or two kinds of difficult sessions to discuss.

### 2. PROPOSAL

Proposals are reviewed by a group of people who usually decide whether to accept, reject, or accept with suggested changes. These suggestions are included when you are informed about your proposal's status.

Most conferences have a form for proposals, and many encourage people to send them online. A proposal typically includes the following information:

- An informative title that tells attendees the gist of your presentation. Avoid vague titles, like "The Flavor of Tutoring," for they tell attendees nothing about your presentation.

- Names, addresses, phone numbers, e-mail addresses, and institutional affiliations for all presenters.

- An abstract that explains the focus of your presentation in a few sentences. Often these abstracts appear in the program and attendees use them to decide which presentations interest them.

- A description of your presentation that adheres to the prescribed length. If your presentation includes several presenters, you may be asked to explain each individual's contribution. Be aware that reviewers of proposals come from other writing centers, so use terms that others will understand. Terms that have meaning in your writing center may be a mystery to someone else.

- Any audiovisual equipment that you will require.

## 3. BEFORE YOU PRESENT

Once your proposal has been accepted, you will need to decide how your presentation will proceed. Break it down by time, especially if you have multiple speakers or plan to involve the audience in activities and feedback. You might allow five minutes for an introduction, ten minutes for an activity, ten minutes for discussion, ten minutes for a second activity, followed by ten minutes for another discussion, and five minutes for questions.

Remember that institutions differ. Don't assume that all writing centers are alike. You might need to give some background and explain that your writing center is open only evenings in dorms or operates only on a walk-in basis or serves mostly older, nontraditional students. If your center goes by a name that might be unfamiliar to your audience, like "the Annex" or "the Write Place," explain that so your references to it won't be confusing. Remember, too, that course numbers and names differ from school to school. What you familiarly refer to as ENGL 101 may be English 110 or Composition 160 somewhere else, so use terminology that everyone will recognize, such as "the first year writing course."

Be sure to have a backup plan for technical glitches. If your salient points or relevant quotations will be presented using an overhead projector or PowerPoint, prepare handouts that you can use if the equipment fails. Bring at least enough copies so that people can share, and be sure to have hard copies of everything for yourself. On any handouts that you provide for participants, make sure that you include the title of your talk, your name, and your e-mail address so that participants can contact you later.

So that you are familiar with it, practice your presentation, preferably before an audience. Time it so that you know whether you can fit everything into the allotted time frame. Get feedback and make adjustments.

## 4. PRESENTING

When you arrive at the conference, check in at the registration table, where you will receive a program, name tag, and other pertinent information. If you can, check out the physical setup of the room where you will be presenting. Will you be speaking from a podium? From behind a table? Are seats for the audience fixed or movable? Troubleshoot and make last-minute adjustments, if necessary. For example, fixed seats may not work well for a planned group activity, so you may want to have people work in pairs instead. If you plan to use electronic equipment like an overhead projector or a computer, check the equipment. Is it in working order and compatible with your material? Where is it positioned? Would it be helpful to have someone else change transparencies or operate the computer for you?

All presenters, even experienced ones, are nervous, which often means that they tend to talk quickly: Before you begin, take a deep breath and remind yourself to speak slowly. Often, several people presenting on similar topics are grouped together for a session; thus, when you present or during the question-answer time, you may be able to refer to parts of the other presentations. As others speak, keep a pen and paper handy to jot down notes that you might later use as you refer to those links.

People often wander in and out during a presentation, especially if two or three presentations are grouped together as a panel. This is acceptable, and you should not consider it an affront to you or your presentation.

## 5. CHAIRING A SESSION

Chairing a session usually means introducing speakers, keeping track of time, and moderating questions, but it may involve only some of these activities. Ask the presenters how they wish to be introduced. Often, a panel prefers to do its own introductions, so you may only need to introduce the session. If there are several speakers, who are each allotted a set amount of time, warn them when they have five minutes then one minute left to speak. Position yourself so that you can unobtrusively show the speaker written warnings that say "5 min." and "1 min." When you moderate questions, be aware of the session's ending time so that people can move to another session and the next presenters can get ready. A gracious way to end is to say, "We have time for one more question." Remember to thank the presenters as you end the session.

# Appendix D

## Outside Tutoring and Editing Jobs

Often, people or companies contact writing centers or individuals in search of private tutors or editors. Following are some suggestions for dealing with prospective employers.

### 1. NEGOTIATING THE PROFESSIONAL RELATIONSHIP

You are a professional who is being paid not only for the work you do but also for your experience, professional training, and level of education. Because you already tutor in a writing center, for a company, or privately, you have a certain amount of professional credence. Don't sell yourself short!

Pay is probably not the first matter you want to discuss—not because it is bad form, but because in order to discuss pay intelligently and fairly, you should know certain details about the job.

#### Questions about Tutoring Jobs

- How much preparation time will be required (for planning, gathering materials, talking to instructors, and so on)?
- Are you responsible for planning the tutoring agenda, or will it be set by an outside source (teachers, SAT preparation books, and so on)?
- Will you be reading papers or reviewing exercises? (The former usually takes more time.)
- How often will you be meeting with the student? For what duration will you be meeting with the student (throughout the semester, over the summer, etc.)?
- What is the student's skill level? Does he or she have any special needs or problems?
- Has the student worked with a tutor before? What was and was not accomplished?
- What are the major goals of the person(s) hiring you?

### Questions about Editing Jobs

- What, precisely, does the employer expect you to do? Some people may say that they simply need help "proofreading" when they actually want you to do major rewriting. You will need to determine if the job entails copyediting (tightening and clarifying sentences, fixing grammatical errors, and so on) or major revision (basically, rewriting the text into understandable English). Ask to be sent several pages of text so you can assess the level and amount of work that will be involved.

- How will the editing be done—by hand on a manuscript or at a computer?

- Is typing the manuscript (as well as editing it) involved?

- Will you be expected to use your own computer, paper, or other supplies?

- How much freedom will you be given? Can you edit on your own, or will you have to work closely with the writer?

- What sort of timetable does the writer expect? Does she or he want you to send portions as you complete them or the entire text upon completion?

## 2. NEGOTIATING PAY

To help determine what to charge, talk to others who also tutor or edit privately. What do their jobs entail with respect to the details listed above, and how much do they charge? You may also call or visit tutoring or editing agencies in your geographic area to obtain the going rate.

Before you accept an editing job, make sure that both you and your employer are in agreement about whether you will be paid according to the time you spend on the text or according to the total number of pages. Some editors charge per hour; others charge a certain amount per page. Whether tutoring or editing, arrange to be paid at regular and frequent intervals (for example, after each tutoring session). Do not allow charges to accumulate. Keep a record of the payment schedule. Show the person paying that you are keeping the record up-to-date by taking it out each time you are paid and noting the payment.

## 3. NEGOTIATING TIME

- For tutoring: In tutoring situations, keep track of time, and try not to go over the limit; if you do, people will tend to expect that you will work longer for them regularly. You cannot expect people to pay for your preparation time, so factor this time into the per-hour rate agreed upon. Also, people do not usually pay for travel time, so take this into account as well.

- For editing: Keep meticulous track of time. The clock should be running from the moment you pick up the work until the time you put it down for the day. If you find that the work is taking more time than you thought, confer with the client.

## 4. ARRANGING MEETING SPACE

If you are tutoring someone, plan to meet at a public place, like a library or a study room on campus. Public places, rather than someone's home, are safer and often more conducive to getting work done. They tend to offer fewer distractions for the person being tutored, and they provide you with greater control over the environment.

## 5. PLANNING FOR THE LONG TERM

- For tutoring: Will you be expected to work toward certain goals (such as helping a student pass an exam)? How much time do you have to meet those goals, and how much responsibility do you have for their successful completion?
- For editing: Will you be expected to work toward certain deadlines? What are they? Will there be rush periods?

# Index

**A**

Abstract for lab report/scientific paper, 89
Academic concerns of students, 56
Accuracy of online sources, 84
Active listening, 22–24
Adult learners, 71–72
Advice template, 85–86
Agenda, setting, 19–21
Ally, tutor as, 28–29
Antagonistic writers, 101
Anxiety, writer's, 61–63
Argument papers, 90
Asking questions in active listening, 24
Assignments
    methods for giving, 12
    reading through, 19–20
Asynchronous tutoring, 17, 74, 76–81
    advantages of, 76–77
    forms of, 76
    tutoring advice for, 77–79
Audience
    global revision and, 9–10
    prewriting and, 9
Auditory learning, 59–60
Authority of online sources, 83–84
Autobiography, writing, 15
Awareness, critical, developing, 26

**B**

Basic writing skills, 63–65
*The Bedford Handbook* (Hacker), 54
    companion Web site for, 81–82
Bias of online sources, 84–85
Body language, active listening and, 23
Book reviews, 91–92
Brainstorming, 42–43
Branching, 44–45
Brooks, Phyllis, 69

**C**

Choppy writing, revision of, 52
Citing sources
    plagiarism and, 69
    research papers and, 88
    Web documents and, 82
Clarification, requesting, 26

Closed questions, 24
Clustering, 45
Coach, tutor as, 29
Code of integrity, plagiarism and, 65, 103–4
Collaborator, tutor as, 29
Commentator, tutor as, 28–29
Comparing writing guides and handbooks, 11
Competency exams, 12
Computers; *see also* Online tutoring
    freewriting and, 43–44
    working with text and, 46–47, 50
Confidentiality, 2
Conversation
    online tutoring and, 76
    second language writers and, 68
    at start of session, 19–20
Council of Writing Program
    Administrators, on plagiarism, 102–3
Counselor, tutor as, 31
Courses, writing, exploring, 11
Cover letters, 96
Critical awareness, developing, 26
Cultural differences, 65
Currency of online sources, 85

**D**

Database systems, asynchronous
    tutoring and, 76
Deadline writers, 99–100
Discussion groups
    International Writing Centers
        Association and, 111
    participating in, 5
Discussion section of lab report/scientific
    paper, 88–89
Documentation
    plagiarism and, 102–4
    research papers and, 87–88

**E**

Editing
    helping student through, 52–54
    as part of writing process, 11–12, 52–54
Elbow, Peter, 7

E-mail, asynchronous tutoring and, 76
Emig, Janet, 7
English as second language, 65–69
*Errors and Expectations* (Shaughnessy),
    63–64
Essays of application, 97–98
Ethics
    plagiarism and, 103
    tutoring and, 1–5
Evidence in argument/position papers, 90
Exercises
    digital age tutoring, 85–86
    getting started, 4–5
    philosophy of tutoring, developing,
        112–14
    references, using, 56–57
    tutoring situations, coping with, 106–10
    tutoring situations, reflecting on, 72–73
    tutoring techniques, practicing, 32–40
    tutors' roles, exploring, 32
    writing process, exploring, 11–13
    writing process, reflecting on, 13–16
Expert, tutor as, 30

**F**
Facilitating tutoring sessions, 21, 24–27
Film reviews, 91–92
Flower, Linda, 7
Freewriting, 8,10, 13, 43–44
Friend, tutor as, 28–29

**G**
Global revisions, 9–10, 48–50
Grade
    disagreeing with, 4
    suggesting, 3
Graduate programs, essays of application
    for, 97–98
Grammar, editing for, 52–54
Guides to writing; *see* Writing guides

**H**
Hacker, Diana, 54
Handbooks
    comparing, 11
    exploring, 56–57
    online, 81–82
    using, 54
Handouts, developing, 56
Harris, Muriel, 29, 53, 67

**I**
Inappropriate topics, 102
Information, requesting, 25–26

Instant messaging, synchronous tutoring
    and, 75
International Writing Centers
    Association, 111–12
Internet phone, synchronous tutoring
    and, 75
Introducing oneself, 18
Introduction of lab report/scientific
    paper, 88–89
"I" statements
    active listening and, 23
    antagonistic writer and, 101
IWCA; *see* International Writing Centers
    Association

**J**
Journal, personal, 4–5

**K**
Keywords, scannable résumés and, 95–96
Kinesthetic learning, 59–60, 60–61
Korean grammar, 66

**L**
Lab reports, 88–89
Last minute writers, 99–100
Learner, tutor as, 30–31
Learning disabilities, 70–71
Learning styles, 59–61
Lifestyle concerns of students, 61
Linear model of writing process, 7–8
Listening, active, 21
Listing, 42–43
Literature papers, 90–91
Long paper
    coping with, 54–55
    writer with, 105–6

**M**
Materials and methods section of lab
    report/scientific paper, 88–89
Mechanics, editing for, 52–54
Murray, Donald, 7

**N**
Negativity
    toward student's writing, 2
    toward teachers, 3

**O**
Offensive language, 102
Online classroom, asynchronous
    tutoring and, 76
Online research, 81–85

Online sources
    accuracy of, 84
    authority of, 83–84
    bias of, 84–85
    citing, 82
    currency of, 85
    evaluating, 82–85
Online tutoring, 74–81
    advice for tutors and, 32, 78–81
    asynchronous tutoring and, 76–81
    clustering and, 45
    global revisions and, 49
    keeping resources handy for, 1
    sentence-level revisions and, 51
    setting the tone and, 1, 18
    stock responses and, 85
    student's control of paper in, 18
    synchronous tutoring and, 75
    texting shorthand and, 2
Online writing guides, 81–82
Online writing resources, 81–85
    videos, 82
    writing guides and handbooks, 81–82
    writing labs (OWLs), 81
Open questions, 24
Outlining, informal, 46

**P**

Paraphrasing, active listening and, 23
"Perfect" paper, improving, 105
Perl, Sondra, 7
Plagiarism, 102–4
    cultural differences of, 69
Play reviews, 91–92
Portfolios, 12
Position papers, 90
PowerPoint presentations, 92–93
Prewriting
    helping student with, 41–47
    tutor strategies and, 38–40
    writing process and, 8–9
Principles of conduct in tutoring, 1–4
Professionalism, 1–4
Prompting with questions, 26
Proofreading, 10–11
Punctuation, editing for, 52–54
Purpose for writing, 8

**Q**

Questioning, active listening and,
    24

**R**

Racist language, 102
Reader, reacting as, 25

Reading paper aloud
    global revisions and, 49
    for grammar and punctuation, 53
Real-time tutoring, 17, 76
References, lab report/scientific paper
    and, 88–89
Refocusing student's writing, 26
Research papers, 87–88
Resources
    keeping handy, 18
    online, 81–85
Result section of lab report/scientific
    paper, 88–89
Résumés, 93–96
Revising
    with computer, 50
    helping student through, 48–57
    as part of writing process, 9–11
Role playing exercises, 33–40, 106–10

**S**

Scannable résumés, 95–96
Scientific papers, 88–89
Seating arrangements, 18
Second language writer, 65–69
    cultural differences and, 65–66
    grammar and, 66, 69
    nonevaluative approach and, 66–67
Sentence-level revisions, 10–11, 51–52
Sexist language, 102
Shaughnessy, Mina, 63–64
Silence, in tutoring session, 21, 27–28
Social concerns of students, 61
Source documentation
    plagiarism and, 102–4
    for research papers, 88
Sources, online; *see* Online sources
Stages of the writing process, 8–11
Stock responses, 78–79, 85–86
    for constructing paragraphs, 79
Student writers, 58–73
    adult learners as, 71–72
    basic writing skills and, 63–65
    concerns of, 61
    English as second language and,
        65–69
    learning disabilities and, 70–71
    learning styles of, 59–61
    personas, role playing and, 33–38
    professionalism toward, 1–2
    refocusing and, 26
    rough drafts and, 58–59
    second language writers as, 65–69
    writing anxiety and, 61–63
Syllabi, exploring, 11–12

Synchronous tutoring, 17, 74–75
    finding and exploring topic in, 45
    forms of, 75

**T**

Teachers, professionalism toward, 3–4
*Teaching One-to-One: The Writing
    Conference* (Harris), 53
Technology
    availability of, 12, 74
    face-to-face at computer and, 75–76
    online tutoring and, 74–81; *see also*
        Online tutoring
Templates, online tutoring and, 78–79,
    85, 86
Terminology, common, 12–13
Textbooks, exploring, 11
Thesis, drafting, 46
Thinking time, 21, 27–28
Title page of lab report/scientific
    paper, 88–89
"to be" verb forms, revision of, 52
Topic, finding and exploring, 41–45
Topic sentence, drafting, 46
Training videos, 82
Tutoring, reflecting on, 16
Tutoring journal, 4–5
Tutoring session, 17–40
    active listening in, 21, 22–24
    exercises for, 32–40
    facilitating, 21, 24–27
    observing, 32
    roles of tutors and, 28–31
    setting agenda for, 19–21
    silence and wait time in, 21, 27–28
    starting, 17–18
    wrapping up, 28
Tutor observation sheet, 34
Tutors
    boundaries, setting, and, 31
    professionalism toward other, 2–3
    roles of, 28–31
    welcoming manner and, 1, 17–18
Tutor training videos, 82

**U**

Undergraduate programs, essays of
    application for, 97
University of Maryland University
    College Effective Writing Center,
    13, 78–79

Unresponsive writers, 100

**V**

Video conferencing, synchronous
    tutoring and, 75
Videos, training, 82
Visual learning, 59–60

**W**

Wait time, 21, 27–28
WCenter, 111
Webbing, 44–45
Web-immersive environments,
    synchronous tutoring and, 75
Web page elements, 82–83
Wordiness, revision of, 20, 50–51, 52
Word processing programs, for revising,
    50–51
World Wide Web sources; *see* Online
    sources
Writers, student; *see* Student writers
Writing center, 1–5
*Writing Center Journal*, 111
Writing expert, tutor as, 30
Writing guides
    comparing, 11
    online, 81–82
Writing-intensive courses, 12
*Writing Lab Newsletter*, 111
Writing process, 6–16, 41–57
    editing and, 9–11, 52–54
    handbooks and, 54, 56–57
    long paper and, 54–55
    planning to write and, 45–46
    prewriting and, 8–9, 41–47
    reflecting on, 14–15
    revising and, 9–11, 48–52
    sharing and, 15–16
    stages of, 8–11
    talking about, 12–13
    teaching of, 11–12
    writing stage and, 9
Writing resources
    keeping handy, 18
    online, 81–85
Writing stage, 9

**Z**

Zinsser, William, 8